Crusade in Spain

Crusade in Spain

JASON GURNEY

FABER AND FABER LTD
3 Queen Square, London

First published in 1974
by Faber and Faber Limited
3 Queen Square London WC1
Printed in Great Britain by
The Bowering Press Plymouth
All rights reserved

ISBN 0 571 10310 3

Contents

MAPS

Plates

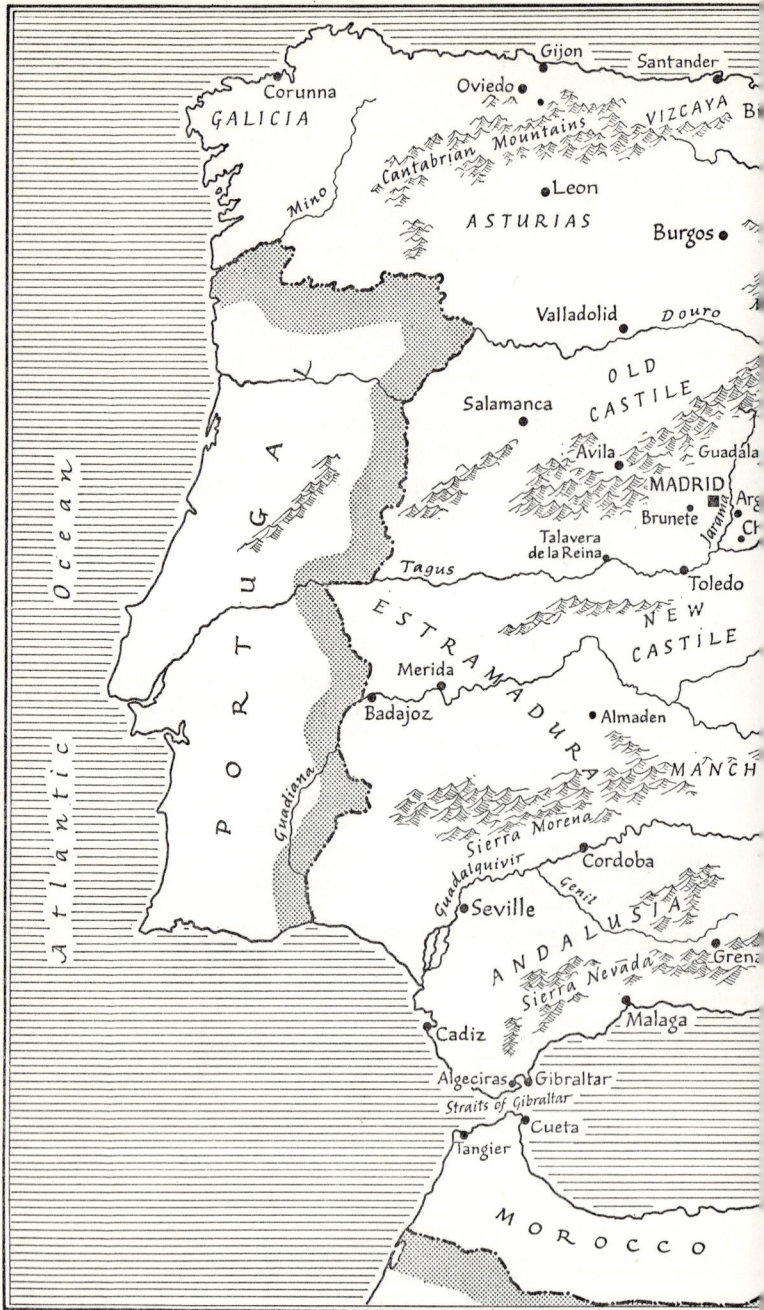

Spain

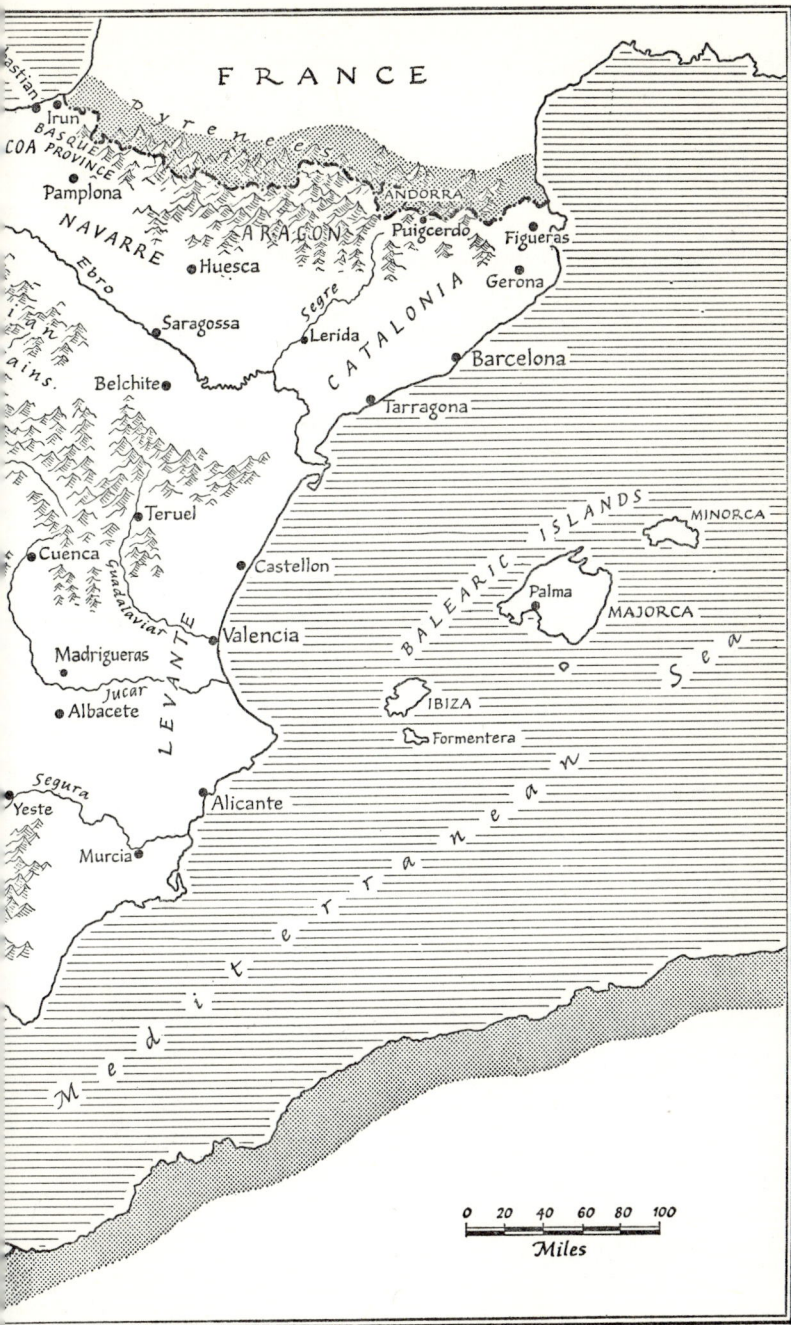

FRANCE

Pyrenees

Sebastian

Irun

BASQUE

COA PROVINCE

Pamplona

NAVARRE

Ebro

Huesca

ARAGON

ANDORRA

Puigcerdo

Figueras

Gerona

Segre

Saragossa

Lerida

CATALONIA

Belchite

Barcelona

ntains

Tarragona

Teruel

BALEARIC ISLANDS

MINORCA

Cuenca

Castellon

Palma

MAJORCA

Guadalaviar

Valencia

Madrigueras

Jucar

IBIZA

LEVANTE

Albacete

Formentera

Segura

Alicante

Sea

Yeste

Murcia

Mediterranean

0   20   40   60   80   100

Miles

Preface

Most personal experiences of the Spanish Civil War were set down during or immediately after the event, usually by dedicated Communists or by ex-Communists who had quarrelled with the Party or became disillusioned. Under these circumstances, it was inevitable that their writing was heavily coloured by a wish to make propaganda or as an apologia for their actions. A large part of this writing was a farrago of nonsense which has, nevertheless, passed into the mythology of the war as established fact.

My own experience of the war lasted only from December 1936 until August of the following year, but was sufficiently typical to give a fairly accurate idea of the nature of that ordeal. Of the 40,000 men from all over the world who fought in the International Brigades, about one-third were killed and a great number were permanently injured. The vast majority of them went to Spain of their own free will to fight for what they believed to be a moral principle. They were offered no reward other than the satisfaction of their own principles, and they suffered horribly.

Thirty-six years later, the question of whether our principles were right or wrong is of little more than academic interest. But an act of altruism on such a tremendous scale deserves to be better understood and I have tried to set down my personal experience of the period as accurately and objectively as possible. Politically I am still no more than an old-fashioned radical and I am too old to have any personal axe to grind. I can only hope that what I have written will contribute to a better understanding of what took place at that time.

Introduction:
A Very Odd Crusade

In February 1936 there was a general election in Spain. The Popular Front alliance won a victory over the National Front. But all this represented nothing at all. The whole country was divided and sub-divided by so many different lines of allegiance that no single individual or party could claim a sufficient degree of support to form a stable government. On the right there were two Royalist parties of almost equal strength. One supported the Bourbon succession, the other the Carlist, and between them there existed no possibility of compromise or agreement. There were two Fascist parties, equally incapable of compromise. There were parties that represented the totally divergent interests of business men and of land owners. And there were parties for every shade of conservative. On the other side a variety of parties embodied all degrees of left-wing thought from the Socialists to the mildest of radicals and liberals, but neither of the two great Trades Union Groups, with more than 3,000,000 members between them, were represented, since they were not affiliated to any political party. As an additional complication there was a very substantial party whose only programme was independence for the Basque provinces, and two more parties, one capitalist and the other Socialist, whose aim was Catalan independence.

It was obvious from the start that there could be no stable government under these conditions, and various disorders quickly arose, beginning with a series of strikes and lock-outs all over the country. Political assassinations were carried out by the parties of the extreme left and of the extreme right. The situation degenerated so rapidly that it soon became apparent that any possibility of compromise had already ceased to exist, and in July a pronunciamento aimed at a military take-over of the Government was issued by a group of generals.

There was nothing extraordinary about that. It followed a fairly consistent pattern of Spanish political history. The only extraordinary element in the situation was that the Junta had failed to do its homework in any very efficient manner. The generals who had organized the plot had assumed that they would enjoy the automatic support of the entire military apparatus. Unfortunately, a surprising number of officers, from generals in command of provincial garrisons right on down the line, preferred to remain true to the oath of allegiance which they had taken to defend the Republic. The *coup d'état* had failed and the country was plunged into civil war. In areas where the army had remained loyal, it was supported by an armed militia organized by the Trades Unions. In areas dominated by the insurrectionary generals an armed militia was formed under the aegis of the Fascist and Royalist party supporters. Fighting broke out all over Spain and it was carried on with all the violence, brutality and heroism that was true to the Spanish tradition. The Government appeared to be holding its own until the arrival of General Franco and the Moorish legionaries from Morocco. It was soon apparent that Franco was receiving a substantial amount of support from Mussolini and Hitler and that the conflict had taken on the character of a straight-out fight between a Fascist and a Democratic regime.

In reality, nothing could have been further from the truth. General Franco was no Fascist: he was merely an anachronism. He was prepared to use the Fascist Leagues as long as he needed them, but he had no intention of sharing power with them, since he regarded them as no more than a lot of new-fangled foreign nonsense from abroad. He was prepared to make use of Italian Fascist and German Nazi troops and equipment, but the idea that Hitler or Mussolini should have any say in Spanish affairs, he would not even consider. Above all, he was a Galician with all the cunning for which that race is notorious. Franco was prepared to use any tool that came to hand. He played them all off, one against the other, and left them all impotent. The limit of his vision was National and Catholic, whatever that meant. The Army and the Church were the keepers of the nation's conscience and no political or economic theory was going to be permitted to interfere with that sacred concept.

In the other half of Spain there was absolute chaos. Some areas were controlled by local authorities of mildly liberal intentions and others had been taken over by proletarian revolutionary committees. The central Government had very little influence anywhere. The principal areas of authority were the two great trades unions: the CNT (Confederación Nacional del Trabajo) the Syndicalist Trades Union, and the UGT (Unión General de Trabajadores), the Socialist Trades Union. Neither of them, however, had any parliamentary affiliation.

It now seems incredible that this rather sordid political mess could have formed the background to one of the most deeply-felt ideological crusades in the history of Western Europe. More than 40,000 men from every country in Europe and the Americas made their way to Spain to fight for the Republic and to fight so desperately that more than a third of their number were killed in battle. They came from every class of society and the number of artists, musicians and writers amongst them was out of all proportion to their numbers in any of the societies from which they came. They were offered no reward, monetary or otherwise, except the satisfaction of their own idealism. In terms of numbers alone, it was a movement comparable with the great Christian crusades of mediaeval times. And certainly it was on the whole actuated by higher motives; none of the latter had been untainted by pecuniary ambition and the Fourth Crusade in particular was a record of greed and deceit, as foul as anything in history.

The 40,000 men who actually went to Spain and joined the Republican Army are only one part of the total number of people who felt themselves involved in the whole drama of the War. For every individual who went to Spain, there must have been dozens who wanted to go but were prevented by lack of decision or family obligations. In any case, the whole of the liberal and radical intelligentsia of the West was emotionally involved to a very high degree. There was also, of course, the involvement of working-class movements who saw the thing more pragmatically as typifying their own struggle, but even this did not explain the almost mystical light with which the whole conflict had become invested.

It has been said that we were the victims of a vast propaganda conspiracy and certainly there was propaganda enough – from both sides. None of the news media seemed to be capable of taking any middle ground and both sides were reflected as monsters of evil or masters of heroism, according to the predilection of the publishers. This pattern of hysteria pervaded the whole reporting of the War from start to finish. People were merely using the War to objectify their own neuroses of one sort or another. The forces of the Republic, were 'Loyalists' in the radical press and 'Reds' or 'Communists' in the right-wing publications. General Franco's forces became the 'Nationalists' or the 'Fascists' according to taste. But in essence, everybody outside Spain came to see the conflict as a battle between Nationalism and Communism or Fascism and Democracy according to their own political leanings.

Nobody was concerned with the facts of the situation. The War became a microcosm of all the ideological divisions of the time – freedom and repression, constitutional and arbitrary authority, nationalism and internationalism, the people and the aristocracy, Catholicism and Marxism, and many more. Everyone saw Spain as the epitome of the particular conflict with which they were concerned. It was for this reason that the writers of the western world became so emotionally involved in the Spanish conflict. For myself, and a great number of people like me, it became the great symbol of the struggle between Democracy and Fascism everywhere. I realized perfectly well that the Communists were taking advantage of the opportunities presented by the War to forward their own interests, but if I had to ally myself with them to fight against the ultimate tyranny of Fascism, I would do so, and deal with subsequent problems when the time came.

The Crusade was against the Fascists, who were the Saracens for our generation.

I

Chelsea 1936

It was raining in the King's Road. The shop windows had all been done up early for Christmas but few of the figures in sodden mackintoshes paused to look at them. There wasn't much money about in 1936 and it was a rotten night in any case. Outside the Gaumont Cinema there were a couple of men in Fascist Party uniform, trying to sell copies of *Action*, but they were not very military looking and their hearts didn't seem to be really in it. Further up, by the bus stop, a small man was offering the *Daily Worker*, his thin fanatic's face opening and closing as he called his wares. But it was past the rush-hour and the few people around didn't seem to take much interest.

In those days Chelsea was still a largely slum area, in which most of the rooms were let off as squalid bed-sitters at ten bob a week. What is now Chelsea Square used to be Trafalgar Square, full of hideous, run-down lodging houses. Dovehouse Street was then Arthur Street and was occupied almost exclusively by costers. The whole area around Sloane and Draycott Avenues was a dismal slum of back-to-back houses known as 'Oakum Bay', a reference to the principal prison work of earlier days. But there were several hundred studios, most of them occupied by working artists as they were so cold and derelict that nobody else would have tolerated them. The Chelsea Polytechnic had a flourishing art school and so, with one thing and another, there was a fairly active colony of painters and sculptors, and many young writers were also attracted to the area by its cheapness and general atmosphere. The community of artists and students was not very favourably thought of by the working-class section of the community who regarded us as an immoral and dissolute lot; and the upper-class fringe around Cheyne Row, South Kensington and Sloane Street disapproved of us all.

We lived in a very restricted world and seldom went out of it. There was a truly magnificent restaurant – the Victoria Working-Man's Dining Room – which served liver, bacon, chips and peas for sixpence and a pint mug of tea for twopence. All the shops along the King's Road were geared to approximately the same level of economy. Caletta's Italian Restaurant was a rather more pretentious affair with excellent Italian family cooking where it was possible to get a very fine meal, including wine, for five bob. Most of us cooked at home and did fairly well on it except during one very bad period when we lived almost exclusively on spaghetti. One of the girls went home to her parents in Weybridge for a weekend; the family thought she was looking poorly and sent her to the family doctor for a check-up. He was horrified to discover that she was suffering from scurvy: a disease he had previously imagined to be restricted to sailors in the tropics, deprived of fresh food before the days of refrigeration. It was certainly unthinkable amongst the citizens of Weybridge.

I lived in Chelsea and vaguely saw it as the microcosm of English life. Beyond the World's End pub was a slum area where the working class lived in conditions of great poverty and despair. A high percentage were unemployed and even the ones who did have jobs received such pathetic wages that they were barely richer than those without. Houses which had been built for one family now provided shelter for six, and there seemed to be precious little hope of things improving. The King's Road area seemed to me to be principally inhabited by people like myself – artists, writers, actors, students and young scientists, engineers, architects and others who had just qualified in the professions and were not yet earning very much money. In our world three pounds a week was considered to be reasonably comfortable and ten pounds to be indecent affluence. At the far end of Chelsea, around Sloane Square were the very rich, who lived a life of great elegance with large houses, staffs of servants and magnificent cars. The Communist and Labour Parties had large and active memberships at the poverty-stricken end, and Oswald Mosley established his Fascist barracks in the old Whitehead's College at the other. Under these circumstances it was not surprising that we developed a rather specialized attitude towards the politics of the day.

I was not personally involved with any political party. I was a working sculptor and just making a sufficient living to keep going on the fairly marginal standard to which I had trained myself. I worked hard all day and spent the nights drinking with my friends and making love. I could eat for half-a-crown a day. I spent nothing on clothes: a pair of jeans, a cotton singlet and a seaman's guernsey were all that I ordinarily wore. A pint of bitter cost eightpence and five bob was enough to buy as much as I could stomach. Chelsea seemed full of interesting and amusing people and of splendid women. I was absorbed in my work and almost totally happy.

Politically speaking, I saw things in simple, radical terms. I hated the poverty and wretched conditions of life at one end of the King's Road and the callous indifference of the rich around Sloane Square. My political interests dated back to the time when I was fourteen. I had spent the afternoon wandering alone on the beach at Sheringham. As I came off the promenade, on my way home, I noticed a little man standing on a soap-box and addressing an audience of half-a-dozen people. He was not a very inspiring figure: straggling moustache, dressed in a bowler hat and a shapeless overcoat. His voice was very mild and he had no art of delivery, but he was obviously filled with a deep and compassionate sincerity. His theme was simply the old cry for human justice: that there was something bitterly wrong with a society that left a large part of the population in misery and near-starvation, and under which the privileged minority could live in such ludicrous and totally unnecessary affluence. He spoke of the long hours and tedious labour, the appalling struggles of working people to keep themselves decently clean and fed, the never-ending terror of un-employment: of couples who were too old to work ending their days in a work-house. He was an uneducated man and his speech was very simple but I was profoundly moved by what he had to say. I knew enough about the world to realize the truth of it, but had accepted the situation as a natural and immutable ordering of society. He then pro-gressed to a William Morris type of idealist Socialism, where all men would be equal and happy. There was an ample sufficiency of all the good things of life, if only people would find the good will to an even and just system of distribution.

I was a rather solitary boy on the verge of adolescence and I experi-enced all the symptoms of true conversion, in the religious sense of the word. I would give my life to this fine and noble cause of human brotherhood. The whole thing seemed to me to be so incontrovertably right and just. There was no idea in my mind of the working class fighting for their rights or of my helping them to do so. The concept of the brotherhood of man was infinitely higher than the squalid bickering over purely material considerations. I was convinced that all men should have the opportunity to live in freedom and in dignity. That material considerations entered into this condition was obvious, but they were secondary. This I later discovered to be the difference between a radical and a Socialist. While it is obvious that there exists a minimum of material well-being below which any sort of dignity and happiness is impossible, it is futile to imagine that a mere redistribution of wealth can bring about the millennium. To reduce the thing to the level of a class struggle was to lose sight of the very purpose for which the struggle was being fought. Even at the age of fourteen it was apparent to me that wealth and happiness are not synonymous, although it took many years for me to realize the implication of this fact. The fight against poverty was the immediate cause and I, too, became a Socialist. The gospel must be preached, the ignorant converted and the unjust brought to book. When I arrived home and announced to my family that I had become a Socialist, they nearly went mad. My aberration was ascribed to various causes ranging from adolescence, through innate vice, to the fact that my grandfather had been an artist, that I was partly French and that I had a Jewish great-grandmother.

I became a real, old-fashioned radical. I was convinced that the world could and should be a wonderful, glorious and happy place; it was only the greed and stupidity of the few that stood in the way. I was a voracious reader. Christianity offered me nothing as I was too bitterly aware of all the hypocrisy and sham which went with it. I did better with the oriental religions, as I was unaware that they were equally beset with humbug and dishonesty. I vividly remember reading Thomas Rhys David's *Early Buddhism* and for a while thought that I was getting somewhere. William Morris's *News from Nowhere* seemed, on first reading, to be a major revelation. The discovery of Kropotkin with *The Conquest of Bread* and *Factories, Fields and Workshops* impressed me deeply. I became obsessed with psychology: surely in this science of the human mind must lie the solution to man's problems? Unfortunately the psychologists seemed to create more problems than they solved and their turgid prose made me depressed and introspective. Since I was completely uneducated my reading was entirely disorganized and erratic. I tried to read *Das Kapital*, but even in Strachey's abbreviated edition I found it incomprehensible. In fact, I have only met one man who has succeeded in getting the whole way through it, but he had spent seven years in the Leavenworth Penitentiary and claimed to have read it from cover to cover three times during his sentence. He went in as a bank robber and came out as a Communist, though I doubt whether the Federal Government thought this much of an improvement. The only piece of Marxist literature that really impressed itself on my mind was the *Communist Manifesto* prepared by Marx and Engels in 1848. This short and simple essay in Marx's theory of the evolution of social structures impressed me as sound argument, but the rest of the Marxist corpus was either incomprehensible to me or appeared to be mere propaganda.

My reading kept me in a constant state of excitement and anticipation. Like most untrained minds, I was obsessed with the idea that the solution of all problems and difficulties lay in one simple package, if only I could discover it. The Labour Party in the thirties was so utterly discredited that I felt it had nothing to offer me. Ramsay Macdonald and his generation had either been corrupted by power or had fallen into a mass of bumbling absurdity, and, at that time, the Attlee generation did not seem to be much better. We all had a tremendous admiration for the energy and initiative of the Communist Party. Indeed, looking back on that period now, it seems fantastic that the Communist Party in England was able to present itself as the defender of the humanitarian cause, at a time when the Stalinist excesses were at their height in the USSR. But there was very little hard news about Russia easily available and any unfavourable reports were put down by us to Tory misrepresentation. In reality we were simply believing what we wanted to believe and rejecting everything else.

In practice, however, we could find no place in the local Party branch. They were tremendously bureaucratic and earnest to the point of absurdity, so that any hint of levity was treated like farting in church. In addition they were always right. There were never two ways about anything. They had studied the works of Marx, Engels and Lenin, which held the correct answer to any subject under the sun, and that was the end of the matter. Since they believed this as implicitly as any of the most bigoted religious sects believed in their scripture, the Party was not for me, but a large number of my friends did become members. I and many others were content to remain outside as supporters of various of its activities.

The Party as that time was undeniably brilliant at making itself all things to all men with radical inclinations. It succeeded in stirring up a truly fantastic energy and enthusiasm in its members, but its real genius was to provide a world in which a great many otherwise lost and lonely people could find happiness and fulfilment. Within the Party they were given a sense of purpose and the comradeship of being associated in a conspiracy. Thousands of young men and women who had come down from the provinces to seek their fortune in London were ideal material for recruitment. Loneliness, the indifference of Londoners to their unhappiness and the failure to make their mark on the society to which they had aspired produced a chip on their shoulders, but the Party appreciated them and gave them a social milieu which they had badly lacked in the days before they left home. In the local branches everyone was equal as long as they were prepared to work energetically for the cause. Here it was possible to belong, instead of living always as an outsider. Everyone was busy and enthusiastic and felt that they were all making a real impression on the world. Everyone had a title and a function. The chap who sold the *Daily Worker* outside the Underground station was not merely the chap who sold the *Daily Worker* outside the Underground station – he was the assistant Agit. Prop. Sec. of the Branch. He distributed leaflets at meetings and rallies, he went on clandestine wall-chalking expeditions at midnight. He made reports and his superiors listened to him with sympathy and encouragement. At the weekly meetings he proposed resolutions aimed at increasing the sales and readership of the *Worker*, which were then disputed and argued over, as if the world depended on the outcome. It may have been rather futile but it made him feel that he was somebody.

Yet, in spite of all the miseries and sufferings of the working class during the Depression, the Communist Party had never been able to achieve a significant mass membership. Nor had any considerable number of voters been persuaded to support the Party at the polls, and it never boasted more than one Member of Parliament at any one time. Under these circumstances it was nothing more than a pressure group for a small section of the working class. But small as it was, it was immensely energetic and succeeded in achieving a wide measure of control over the Trades Unions, taking advantage of the apathy felt by the majority of the workers. In a factory employing 5,000 workmen it was common for only ten to turn up for a works meeting of their Union, and eight of these were likely to be Party members. The betrayals of Ramsay Macdonald, and of J. H. Thomas – the former general secretary of the National Union of Railwaymen who had enjoyed great popularity at one time, but had supported the National Government of 1931 – and others had destroyed confidence in the Labour Party and the Trades Union movement amongst the mass of members, and frequently a handful of Party members were able to elect each other into control of the entire structure.

Russia was painfully aware that Hitler's *jehad* against Communism would sooner or later culminate in an invasion of the USSR, and the Communist Parties in all countries outside Russia were one of her most valuable weapons. In face of the emergency, the movement temporarily abandoned the dream of World Revolution and the various Parties were reorganized in such a way that they might increase their power to impose extreme pressure on their own governments. One technique which was employed was the formation of what later came to be known as Communist Front organizations. Party members were instructed to join any 'protest' organization – the Peace-pledge Union, the League of Nations Union, Committees for the Protection of Negroes in Africa, of Hindus in India, or of Jews in Germany. There were Associations of Writers, Artists, Surgeons, Lawyers or anyone else who wanted to express their favour of reforms or disgust against every known form of abuse. Wherever a committee was lacking, one was quickly formed. The vanity of the famous, or those who aspired to fame, was flattered into putting their name to one or other of a dozen committees. The Communists were indefatigable in them all, but every one of them professed a total autonomy and it was considered essential that they should not appear to be related to the Communist Party. As a result of these activities a large part of the intelligentsia became involved in support of projects which the Party favoured and controlled. In the context of the period this situation was neither remarkable nor absurd. There was so much suffering and misery to protest against, and so few outlets for any effective action, that these committees at least gave the illusion of being able to do something to prevent the drift into Fascism and war. The technique of building up this huge edifice of organizations which, while apparently non-Communist, would support any line that the Party was pursuing, depended on being able to parade a considerable body of influential and respected persons who were not identifiable as Party members, nor even as politically-attached people.

It would be ridiculous to suppose that of all the young men of wealthy and influential families, the Communists only succeeded in recruiting Philby, Burgess and Maclean. At this time, it was an open secret that Communist Party members in influential positions were prohibited by the Party from declaring their membership or from open involvement in Party activities. In reality there was practically no form of public enterprise or organization that was not infiltrated at every level by people who accepted the Party directive. All branches of scientific and technical associations had Party members secretly agitating in support of policies approved by the Communists. Newspaper staffs – including *The Times* – were infiltrated by Party members whose function was to attempt to 'angle' the news as far as it was possible to do so without showing themselves as overt supporters. The Civil Service was also infiltrated – as we now know – up to the highest levels of the intelligence service. The names of those involved in these underground activities on behalf of the Communist Party have been successfully buried in most cases, but during the 'cold war' years there must have been some bitter soul-searching amongst many people who had now arisen to places of great power and influence.

The despair we felt at our inability to control our own destinies was not concerned solely with the rise of Fascism throughout Europe and the danger of it in our own country; the Depression had proved to us that the ruling class could not control the system it had itself produced. It had not suffered as had the working class; but by its own standards it had suffered very considerably and had not been able to protect itself against the ravages of an inadequate system of distribution and exchange. It was indeed fortunate for the ruling class that the threat of war, followed by its reality, saved the country from collapse and revolution.

This may seem exaggerated but it was mainly the expansion of the 'defence' industries that arrested the progress of the Depression. Whether a Socialist system would be any more successful, or how such a system could be successfully applied was then a matter for speculation only, as there appeared to be no way in which it could be instituted. England would have to go a long way farther down the drain before a revolution took place, and when it did take place it was much more likely to be Fascist than Socialist.

Looked at today, it may seem rather far-fetched to have imagined that England was in danger of becoming a Fascist state. But then it appeared to be well within the bounds of possibility. Ever since the General Strike, right-wing politicians and newspapers had constantly screamed of the imminence of Red Revolution. The mutiny of the Fleet at Invergordon and the use of the Army against strikers in South Wales together with a host of minor events of a similar kind had fostered the idea. The publication in 1924 of the Zinoviev letter, supposed to contain instructions to British Communists for all sorts of seditious activities, and the raid on the offices of the Soviet trading organization at Arcos House in London in May, 1927 had led many people to believe that there was a vast conspiracy financed by Russian gold to promote an active revolutionary movement in England. In many countries of Europe, the response to similar situations had resulted in the rise to power of Fascist dictatorships. And, if the bourgeoisie in England had felt themselves in sufficient danger, they might well have favoured the same course. Mosley was no mere illiterate house painter. He was impeccably upper class, a baronet related to many of the greatest families in the land, a product of Winchester and Sandhurst and a very handsome man of outstanding intellectual attainments and considerable wealth. He had been one of the rising stars in both the Tory and the Labour parties. He was a good speaker with many admirers and had intimates in every stratum of the political scene. There were those who considered him over-ambitious or unstable in his allegiances but to many young men of the middle and lower middle classes he appeared as the perfect political leader.

Before Mosley there had been a number of Fascist and National Socialist splinter groups which he amalgamated into the British Union of Fascists, commonly known as the BUF. He took over the old Whitehead's College building in the King's Road, Chelsea, on the site now occupied by Whitehead's Flats, as his general headquarters and barracks. All the personnel wore the official 'blackshirt' uniform: a black upper garment, similar to a fencer's tunic, a wide black leather belt with a large brass buckle, black trousers and black jackboots. The barracks was run on full military lines with sentries at the gate, guard-mounting ceremonies, bugle-calls and all the other paraphernalia. It was a very considerable affair with dormitories, gymnasium, parade ground, offices, a basement converted to prison cells, and a potential establishment of 5,000 persons. There were similar, if smaller, establishments in a number of provincial towns from Bournemouth to Birmingham and beyond.

The movement was given considerable support by a number of newspapers and magazines, particularly the *Daily Mail* and the *Evening News*, which devoted two pages a day exclusively to the Fascist Party. It appears to have had unlimited funds that could not have been derived only from the membership fees of one shilling per week or from Mosley's personal fortune. At its height the organization must have been dispensing at least £100,000 per month and probably very much more. We now know from official sources that a part of this money came from the Italian Fascist Government. Undoubtedly some private individuals gave substantial subscriptions but it seems likely that the bulk of money came from British industrial and commercial companies.

Violence was implicit in every aspect of the movement from the day of its foundation. Apart from the para-military character of the whole organization, the system on which meetings were run was deliberately provocative. The speaker would arrive in uniform accompanied by a uniformed escort. As he mounted the rostrum his escort would greet him with the Fascist salute and then form up in front of him, facing the audience, and assume a truculent attitude. The speaker would then warn his audience that any attempt to disrupt the meeting would be met by force, and frequently it was. This technique reached its height at one of Mosley's biggest demonstrations at Olympia. 15,000 tickets were sold, mostly through the theatre ticket booking agencies, with considerable publicity engineered through the *Daily Mail* and the rest of the Rothermere press. A phalanx of uniformed Fascists filled the steps of the main entrance and the hallway, checking tickets and frisking suspected members of the public. The aisles of the hall were lined with other members, whose function soon became apparent. Mosley appeared to a fanfare of trumpets and started to make his speech. Before he had completed his first sentence someone in the audience got up and shouted a protest. Mosley immediately stopped speaking, a spotlight picked up the offender in the darkened hall, and a body of stewards ran in, beat him up and carried him outside. This process continued for more than two hours. Outside the hall there was an opposition meeting of 10,000 protestors, with a force of 700 foot and mounted policemen attempting to keep the two factions apart. The atmosphere became increasingly tense as the interrupters were ejected: many of them showing clearly the injuries which they had suffered. The whole affair was not finally over before the early hours of the morning.

Another form of aggression popular with the Fascist Party was to march through the areas where opposition to them was strongest. The purpose was to demonstrate that they had the mastery of the streets, in emulation of the SS in Germany, and one of the alarming aspects of the marches was that the Fascists were able to demonstrate that they had police support. The official view was that anybody had the right to hold meetings or processions without interference, but to the man in the street it only appeared that the police were on the side of the Fascists. The marches followed the pattern of the Nazi Party with the 'Leader' in an open car escorted by a dozen, uniformed outriders on motor cycles. Next came a squadron of Division I members – the strong-arm section – in black uniforms with breeches and jackboots. They were followed by the band and the ordinary members in black shirts and black trousers, while the 'armoured car squad' brought up the rear. The most alarming incidents occurred when an attempt was made to march through the East End of London, which at that time was the centre of London's Jewry and a militant working-class area. Sir Philip Game, the Chief Commissioner of the Metropolitan Police, mobilized 600 foot policemen and the whole of the mounted section to escort the march. The centre of opposition was in Cable Street, off the Whitechapel Road. Here the crowd battled with the police throughout the afternoon, building barricades and resisting a series of baton charges. Tempers became increasingly enraged and the fighting more and more ugly. Finally Sir Philip, in consultation with Sir John Simon at the Home Office, agreed that the situation had become intolerable and persuaded Mosley to call off the march.

I had been an observer of all this in the year preceding the Spanish Civil War. I had seen the hatred and violence, with the resulting pattern of fear it introduced into the lives of ordinary men, and I hated the whole thing. People were becoming increasingly irrational in their attitudes as they became increasingly powerless to arrest the drift towards potential civil war. My attitude may be hard to believe today, but we had seen what had happened in Germany. There, too, people had laughed off Hitler and the Nazi Party until they had found themselves overwhelmed by the situation and the Nazis had become the masters of the German state. Fascism was strengthening its hand in every country in Europe and those who felt strongly about it, and took no action to stop it, experienced a very real sense of guilt.

The war in Spain had started at a time when the apparent danger of Mosley's Fascist movement was at its height, and produced a wave of emotion in England similar to the Philhellenism at the time of the Greek War of Independence. I think that this strong element of emotionalism was largely produced by one's sense of being powerless to do anything about the rise of Fascism. The Spanish people were fighting desperately and with considerable courage for the freedom in which they believed, and their courage was, in a sense, a reproach to those in England who saw the danger but did nothing to avert it. With the benefit of hindsight it is very easy to argue that we were wrong and foolish, but in the context of the period it seemed entirely reasonable.

2

Bohemia Prepares for War: King's Road to King Street

As far as I personally was concerned, I was a sculptor; twenty-six years of age and just at the point where I was building a small reputation and earning sufficient money to live in what I considered to be reasonable comfort. I had started work in Johannesburg under a very old, very good academic sculptor called Van Wouw. But the Depression years in South Africa had been extremely hard. Eventually I had the good fortune to find employment in the Norwegian whaling fleet and had saved up enough money to come to Europe. I had worked in Paris with Ossip Zadkine and in London with Frank Dobson. The fact that I was exceedingly large and powerfully built helped me considerably. The donkey work of roughing-out large carvings in wood or stone for other people was never a hardship for me. On the other hand it gave me an opportunity to work on larger pieces of material than I could have afforded for myself.

I honestly don't know how good a sculptor I was. I have no doubt that I produced at least three important pieces. I was a good craftsman in wood or stone but never achieved the delicacy of touch which I sought as a modeller. I worked obsessively and sculpture was the principal interest of my life, but the work derived from an equally strong obsession with people. For me, the human body was an unending source of delight. I spent hours stripped naked in front of a mirror, with a drawing board on one side and an anatomy book on the other, moving the various bones and muscles of my body, studying exactly how the whole thing worked. I was fascinated by the perfection of the mechanics of the structure, and the elegant logic by which the bones and muscles worked on one another to produce any given movement. In spite of this purely technical interest in anatomy, I did not want to produce academic or photographic sculpture, but sought to convey the elegance of the form by implication rather than direct statement. I was very much influenced by Egyptian and negro sculpture with the severe classicism which both possessed. It seemed to me that a sculpture should not be a mere recording of one particular person or event but should be a statement which was concerned with all human bodies at all times. I was interested in abstraction in a general sort of way and produced a large number of abstract drawings and a few small abstract sculptures, but this I regarded more as a game which was tremendous fun but not of any real importance.

Given this obsession with the human body, it was not unnatural that I should have delighted so completely in sex. For me it was the logical outcome of everything that was wonderful and beautiful about the human body. I had a studio just off Manresa Road. It didn't have a bathroom or kitchen and the roof leaked in two places when it rained, but it had plenty of space and light. It opened onto a big yard, shared by three other studios. We were all sculptors, and I at least thought it was very beautiful. I had a girl friend who had the most glorious body I have ever seen. She was a bad model, because she couldn't keep still and frequently started to get sexy when I wanted to draw, but I loved her dearly and never tired of looking at her. She had blonde hair, tight-curled like a negro's, which stood up in a tremendous shock except when held down with a rubber band. A high, rather narrow forehead with the line that the Greeks so dearly loved: straight and unfaltering from the peak of the forehead to the tip of the nose. A long neck in which every muscle was faintly visible as they ran down into the structure of the thorax. Broad shoulders to set off a pair of small, hard but perfect pear-shaped breasts which pointed outwards from one another, giving them a magnificently arrogant appearance. A high diaphragm and below that, the faintly visible mass of the abdominal muscles. This ran into a pelvis, set very erect so that her back was as straight as a male athlete, with long, fine-drawn dancer's legs. The real glory was a very fine layer of fat under the skin, so that while every detail of her anatomy was identifiable, it always remained subtle and never became angular, and I never tired of looking at it. During the previous summer I did one high-relief, life-size sculpture of her, one bust and dozens of drawings. I never saw her in the evenings as she was playing in the chorus of a show in the West End and slept in the chorus girls' hostel in Greek Street. We spent the days together and I had an entirely separate life after six. During the day I worked and made love; in the evening I went out drinking and talking endlessly with my friends, usually starting at the Six Bells and Bowling Green in the King's Road.

The Bells at that time was still a very old-fashioned kind of pub. It was run by a little man with waxed moustaches, named Markham. He was reputed to have been the smallest sergeant-major in the British Army, and he certainly behaved that way. He had six barmen in black alpaca jackets who were paraded every morning with their hands held out in front of them for Markham's inspection. No camaraderie between one side of the bar and the other would ever have been permitted. To complete this isolation there was a screen built over the bar, with a space underneath for the barmen to pass the drinks and a series of small panels which could be opened by the customer to give his order. In summer the doors at the far end were opened onto a terrace facing out over the bowling green. The bar was about fifty yards long and only about six feet wide on the customer's side. But in spite of its generally depressing character, the Six Bells and Bowling Green was the acknowledged centre of Chelsea's Bohemia. Painters and sculptors, writers and undiscovered actors, students from the Chelsea School of Arts, poets and the usual dilettante of the art world all used the Bells as their central meeting place. Dylan Thomas was an *habitué*. So were Rex Harrison who was always immaculate but, as yet, penniless, and Leslie Charteris, who had still to make his fortune with the 'Saint'. Betty May, one of Epstein's models who wrote her autobiography *The Tiger Woman* which involved her in one of the most fantastic libel suits in history; Lionel Leslie, a sculpture and nephew of Winston Churchill; Stanley Grimm, a Russian painter and doyen of the White Russian colony in Chelsea. A painter who, in spite of being deaf and dumb, could always carry on a most amusing conversation by means of sketches and written comments. A great number of young women students, models or merely hangers-on. To a twenty-six-year-old sculptor from the Colonies, it was paradise.

After the Six Bells closed at ten o'clock we would go on to one of several small drinking clubs, and usually there was a party somewhere around. If we were in a more serious mood we went to Ye Olde Chelsea Cooke Shoppe. This was a sleazy basement in the King's Road, run by a short but remarkably spherical old girl, reputed to be a retired female weight-lifter from the circus. She ran the place on a very strict 'no bloody nonsense' basis and everyone treated her with grave respect. She was herself no respecter of persons and the rough side of her tongue was very rough indeed. The menu was restricted to eggs – boiled or fried – bacon, sausages, toast and tea, and strangers were firmly discouraged. She lived in the backroom and cannot have made much money out of the business. But in her own way she was very fond of us and had no life outside the place. Apart from the regular writers and poets, with two or three painters and sculptors, there was an economist, and a salesman from Tooth's Art gallery who later became notorious as 'Buster' Crabbe, the frogman. A few girls were allowed in but we were a predominantly male company, in our middle twenties. It was more like a debating society than a café. We had discussions on philosophy, politics and a variety of other subjects, but in the end everything came back to politics. In retrospect, it seems odd that I should have spent half my time roaring around the clubs and parties in a welter of drink, sex and nonsense while the other half was spent in this intensely serious atmosphere of politics and philosophy.

There used to be a party in one or other of the studios every Saturday evening and frequently in between. One or more quart bottles of beer was the entry fee, but a quart only cost one and sixpence, which was not prohibitive. The orgiastic nature of these studio parties has been ridiculously exaggerated; largely by their participants. We liked to think that we were wildly gay and untrammelled by bourgeois convention, but in reality there was not much serious drunkenness, simply because we could not afford it. The sexuality would have been considered very mild by modern standards. Fights took place quite frequently with a great deal of sound and fury, but very little damage was done. The party usually consisted of a large number of people sitting on the floor, in a dim light, necking or arguing art and politics, with a few couples dancing to the music of an old gramophone. The drink usually ran out by two o'clock and people drifted off, leaving only the hard-core of political debaters who required no alcoholic stimulus.

Chelsea was always well provided with an apparently unlimited supply of young women. They came in all shapes and sizes and degrees of attraction. A great many came from the provinces to escape the attentions of censorious parents, attracted to Chelsea by its reputation for permissive Bohemianism. The majority of them soon tired of the dirt and discomfort of a poverty-stricken life and settled for a good, solid, bourgeois marriage, while treasuring the memories of a year spent in exploring the beds of Bohemia. At that time the Chelsea School of Art at the Polytechnic was one of the largest and most flourishing in the country. Many of the students from the Royal Colleges of Art, Music and so on in South Kensington preferred to live in Chelsea, as did many from the various establishments of London University. Apart from the artists and students there were a number of writers and journalists. Added to this was a group of political refugees from all over Europe, and taken all in all, it was a fairly lively community with very few inhibitions about the way its members conducted their private lives.

As I identified sex with sculpture, I identified conviviality – my other prime delight – with politics. I have always enjoyed people *en masse* – pubs, clubs, parties and any other assemblage of people who are there to enjoy one another's company. As long as they are cheerful, or amusing, or interesting, or participating in the general feeling of the group I am prepared not to be too critical. It would be ridiculous to expect all men to be intelligent or possessed of a great sense of humour or even to be totally honest, but there is a level of social life where they can meet and enjoy the best of one another. It is only a matter of good will amongst men. Either to love one's fellow man or to wish to dominate and to exploit him – these seemed to me to be the two sides of the political coin: the rest was humbug and hypocrisy.

It was obvious that this state of happy-go-lucky Bohemia could not last for ever. Hitler had stated quite clearly in *Mein Kampf* that his programme was the subjugation of the whole of Europe and there was plenty of evidence that he really meant it. There was no longer any doubt that war was coming: the only question was when it would break out. The British Government wobbled from one crisis to another and the whole of Europe lived in a continuous state of anxiety. The Labour

Party's only contribution towards a solution was a call for disarmament and support of 'collective security' under the League of Nations which had already proved itself totally ineffective in the comparatively minor affair of the Italian invasion of Ethiopia. A terrible frustration was induced by our being forced to sit idly by and watch the smaller nations of Europe being destroyed one by one, and see all the principles for which we stood being totally submerged.

The Spanish Civil War seemed to provide the chance for a single individual to take a positive and effective stand on an issue which appeared to be absolutely clear. Either you were opposed to the growth of Fascism and went out to fight against it, or you acquiesced in its crimes and were guilty of permitting its growth. There were many people who claimed that it was a foreign quarrel and that nobody other than Spaniards should involve themselves in it, but for myself and many others like me it was a war of principle, and principles do not have national boundaries. By fighting against Fascism in Spain we would be fighting against it in our own country, and every other. We felt that the victory of Fascism was inevitable. Mussolini had triumphed overnight, Hitler appeared to be irresistible, and there were similar leaders throughout the world.

In December 1936 I therefore decided I had a positive duty to go to Spain and join the International Brigades, who were already playing their part in the defence of Madrid against the army of General Franco. This was not a political decision but a question of my own personal integrity as a man. For several years I had been deeply concerned in the current pattern of radicalism. I had professed certain convictions and felt that it would be dishonourable not to fight for them now that an opportunity presented itself. I am convinced that this was not an unusual or eccentric position, at that particular moment. The Spanish Civil War produced a genuine crisis of conscience amongst the radicals of the period. There is no doubt that at this time Leftism had become fashionable at the Universities and amongst intellectuals all over the country. A great number of them were obviously deeply concerned about the condition of national and international affairs, but many of these professed radicals seem to have been inspired either by a desire to be fashionable or to profit from the movement. Too many people were talking too much and I felt that the time had come when any decent man must either put up or shut up. Either I had to shut up – forget about my politics and principles altogether – or I had to join the army in Spain. That I was by no means alone in the agony of this decision was apparent from the deeply traumatic sense of guilt felt by a great number of my friends who decided against going. Subsequently they were constantly explaining the reasons why – that although they had wanted to go they were prevented from doing so. Nobody accused them, but they felt the need to excuse themselves. Even today I frequently meet people who tell me how much they regret that they did not go to Spain.

I had heard a rumour that the Communist Party had opened a recruiting centre at their offices in King Street at the back of Covent Garden market. One morning I made my way down through the chaos of barrows, baskets and trucks until I eventually found the office, huddled between two fruit wholesalers. Up a bare wooden staircase into a maze of small offices with interleading doors and passages. At that time there was a particular type of young woman who seemed irresistibly attracted to the Communist Party. She was usually thin and dark, with stringy black hair and a sallow, oily complexion, and frequently of an exceedingly aggressive and bossy character accompanied by a sneering manner. These women were the truly dedicated and regarded everybody else as charlatans. To support their detachment from everything but the 'cause', they dressed in plainest black and seemed to take pleasure in making themselves as physically unattractive as possible.

After hanging around for some time I cornered one of them and explained that I had come to join the International Brigades. She looked at me as if I was likely to be more of a liability than an asset and told me to wait. There was a terrific flow of people dashing in and out with a great air of purpose and activity, but eventually I was shown up to an office on the top floor and introduced to Comrade Robson who sat at an old-fashioned roll-top desk in a room which contained no other furniture than nine old kitchen chairs. There were only two others present when I arrived and I was instructed to sit down and wait while Robson continued his work in the bowels of the old desk. Within about ten minutes the room had filled up with the addition of another half-dozen. Nobody seemed to know anyone else and we all sat around and fidgeted until Robson finally turned round and delivered himself of a short and rather threatening lecture. He was completely fair and frank in what he had to say. It was a bastard of a war, we would be short of food, medical services and even arms and ammunition. If any of us believed that we were going into a fine adventure we might as well pack up and go home right away. He could promise us nothing but the opportunity to fight Fascism, on the evils of which he enlarged at great length. He then sat back and asked if any of us had any questions. One individual became very insistent about the conditions of service, whereupon Robson snapped at him, 'If you're looking for conditions of service, you're not the kind of bloke we want in Spain. So get out.' This seemed to me to be the right attitude and I was impressed. I was going to regret it later, but at the time it seemed almost indecent to ask conditions for the privilege of serving in a crusade. We were not submitted to any kind of medical examination. Robson asked if we were fit and healthy and took our word for it. We were given twenty-four hours to make our personal arrangements and told to report back at the same time on the following day.

I was now committed. Not in any legal sense – if I had cared to forget about the whole thing, there was nothing that anybody could do about it – but I was committed to my own self in a way that was more total than any legal commitment could ever be. From this moment I was separated from the commonality in the same way as a mediaeval knight who had endured his vigil. I did not see it in these terms at the time, merely that I was now in some sense responsible only to the thing that I had entered, and was divorced from all the immediate things in which I had previously been engaged. I was no longer responsible for the world in which I had always lived.

I went and had tea with my mother. She had done her best to bring me up as a solid member of the English middle class, because she thought it was her duty to do so. But she came of a long line of artists, of assorted nationality, and she never questioned my right to live as I saw fit. Back in Chelsea I determined to make the best of my last night and covered the round of all the familiar places. Everyone wanted to buy me a farewell drink, all my girl friends were sweet and sympathetic, and it was a tremendous evening. The following morning I packed up a few things in a small suitcase and reported back to the office in King Street. The original eight men that I had met on the previous day had now increased to fifteen. They were all working-class fellows about my own age, poorly but respectably dressed; most of them in their Sunday suits, raincoats and cloth-caps. Everybody was very subdued, as we were all strangers to one another. Finally I found myself at Victoria station. I was put in charge as I was the only person with a passport and able to speak French. The rest were travelling on three-day return tickets to Paris which did not at that time require passports. It was cold and drizzling as we found ourselves seats in a couple of third-class compartments. Nobody talked very much as we were all hopelessly unsure of ourselves. We had all been brought up on horror stories of the 1914–18 war and none of us felt too happy about our prospects.

Once aboard the Channel steamer, however, the whole atmosphere changed completely. We had left England and there was no going back on our decision. Like all Englishmen out of England for the first time, my charges proceeded to get drunk and with the release of the tension they became obstreperous. It would be a ghastly anti-climax if the French authorities shipped us all back because these idiots couldn't keep their mouths shut. Besides I was in charge. I had never been in charge of anything before and didn't want to make a mess of my first piece of responsibility. We got ashore without any trouble but there were three hours to wait in Calais before we could get a train to Paris. I tried to keep them all in the same bar so that, drunk or sober, I knew where they all were. They thought that I was being pompous and officious which annoyed me but finally I got them all onto the train where they collapsed. On arrival at the Gare du Nord the taxi-drivers, who were all Red enthusiasts, recognized us immediately for what we were and gave us a free ride to the *Bureaux des Syndicats* which was the assembly place for foreign volunteers coming from all over Europe. I delivered my charges and was free until we were due to entrain for Perpignan on the following evening.

I went to an hotel, slept for a few hours, bathed, shaved and felt normal again. I wanted one last touch with the world in which I had lived, so I rang my old friend Herriot Holmes and his wife who offered to take me out to dinner. They asked me where I wanted to go and I elected for the Rosalie, just around the corner from Bill Hayter's studio in the rue Campagne Premier. This had always been one of my favourite places in the days when I had been studying at the Colorossi, which must surely have been one of the most dilapidated art schools in the world. It was so cold and draughty that the models were always covered in goose-pimples. Their pay was only one shilling per hour, which didn't attract the most beautiful creatures in Paris, but their undernourished-looking bodies, blue with cold, was the most anti-sexual experience imaginable. It was quite some time before I discovered that the female form was not always repellent.

Herriot and Suzanne treated me rather as if I were a man on his way to the scaffold in a good and noble cause. They were both very emotionally involved in the war and, like so many more, Herriot felt a great sense of guilt that he was not coming with me. But he would have made a lousy soldier, whereas he was a good journalist with a lot of influential contacts all over Europe and America, and in some respects Spain needed friends more urgently than soldiers.

In 1936 most of the famous Montparnasse cafés were still closed up as the result of their failure during the Depression – only the Dome and the Select (known as the Homo-Select) were in operation. So after dinner we strolled down to the Dome and drank coffee with Calvados. While we were there I met a number of the characters I had known as a student – the Mexican who looked so much like an Aztec sculpture that he always had plenty of work as a model, but was always broke because he invested all his money on twenty-horse parleys at one or two francs a time. This involved an accumulator bet on twenty successive horses – if they all came up he stood to make several thousand francs but if any one of them failed he lost his original stake. He always had a great number of these bets running simultaneously and was always on the point of making a fortune which never materialized. There was the fantastic, old coquette who always sat in the left-hand corner of the *terrasse*, still living on her reputation of have been Foujita's mistress. An Englishman, dressed as a Russian orthodox priest, who could take a dollar off a tourist quicker than anyone in Montparnasse. There was Gladys who enjoyed a considerable amount of success as a model on the grounds that she was 'the perfect Breton type' – although she came from Cerbére in the Pyrenées Orientales. She had an enormous following among the Americans on the grounds of having been Grant Wood's mistress – Grant was very highly thought of in the States at that time.

These and many others filled me with a great nostalgia for the quarter and a desire to see it all again for the last time. I made some sort of excuse to leave Herriot and Suzanne, who evidently thought that I was going after a woman and were very sympathetic. In reality, my intention was far more innocent. If there were going to be bad times ahead – as I knew there would be – I wanted to fill my mind with happy memories of the past to console me, like an old courtesan with her souvenirs. I just wandered around confirming my memories of places and people that had given me so much happiness in the past.

The departure of the 'Red Train' from the Gare Austerlitz had become one of the sights of Paris. There was no secrecy about the whole affair and crowds with banners came to wave us off. I suppose that there must have been all sorts of people travelling on the Perpignan train but the crowd had no difficulty in picking out the two hundred volunteers of thirty different nationalities who were on their way to Spain. It was rather embarrassing to be treated as heroes before we had done anything and we were delighted when the train finally pulled out. We arrived in Perpignan in the early morning after a terrible night in the cold, overcrowded train. But here it was quite warm and the sun shone as we were led off to an old, ruined château and our first taste of barrack life. There were already about 150 men of different nationalities waiting to cross into Spain, amongst whom was a British contingent of twenty-five who had been hanging around for several days. There did not seem to be any organization or anyone in charge of the place, except a bunch of Frenchmen who were doing a good job running the kitchen. Someone suggested that the British contingent should hold a meeting and try and get ourselves organized. I was elected as the *responsable*. The official language of the International Brigade was French and it appeared that *responsable* was the correct designation of the individual in charge of a detached unit. My election to this office derived from the fact that I was the only one of us with any military experience, and that was limited to the OTC which I had so bitterly detested at school. We divided ourselves into three sections of twelve men, each with a section leader, and set about to learn a bit of squad-drill so that we could put up at least some sort of military appearance and relieve the monotony of hanging around with nothing to do.

It was in Perpignan that I first met 'Tiny' Silverman. He topped my height of six foot two and must have weighed several hundred pounds but, like so many people who are grossly fat, he was tremendously energetic and unfailingly cheerful. Everybody was fond of him, particularly after he became known as the one really conscientious member of the cookhouse staff. He suffered considerably from never being able to get any boots or uniform to fit him, which was a particular hardship for a man who was trying to keep himself clean in a necessarily dirty job. He was one of a group who had come from the Hackney Communist Party. They were all in their twenties and idealists, rather than doctrinaire Communists. I formed an immediate affinity with them and they all remained friends of mine for the whole time that I was in Spain. They were all real Londoners with that greatest of all Cockney characteristics, the ability to retain their sense of humour, even under the worst possible conditions. One of their number, Francis (whose surname I cannot remember), became a very close friend of mine and was later co-opted in to the Battalion scouts. He was the first man wounded at Jarama.

After two days in Perpignan we were loaded onto buses which were to take us over the border to Figueras. The buses arrived at midnight and the whole affair was supposed to be carried out in total secrecy. I succeeded in getting all my three sections into one bus and we set off in darkness and silence. Things were completely uneventful until we reached the French border post. We were stopped at the barrier and I could see various officials moving about with lanterns. Our bus was third in line and all the activity seemed to be taking place at the head of the column. Suddenly one of the fellows at the back of the bus started screaming 'I don't want to go. I don't want to go.' Everybody sat looking at him without doing anything. Our crossing of the border was entirely illegal and although the authorities were conniving at it, they were liable to become excited if there was a major drama. When French officials start to get excited the future always becomes very uncertain and I decided that since I was in charge it was up to me to do something about it. The only way I knew to shut a man up quickly was to belt him. Any sort of a struggle would have made things worse so I hit him on the point of the jaw and he dropped. He cried a lot that night at Figueras but seemed to be quite content thereafter and never held it against me. But when I saw his body lying dead, two months later, on the Jarama fields, I felt like a murderer. It was all very well trying to be a good soldier but it needed a kind of ruthlessness which was not in my nature. I could do the things which it was necessary to do at the time but I always had to pay the price for it in retrospect.

3

Arrival in Spain

The barracks to which we were taken after crossing the border was in a glorious mediaeval castle on the outskirts of the town of Figueras. We occupied a dormitory in the dungeons of the castle which later witnessed one of the most tragic episodes in Spanish history – the last meeting of the Cortes. The Spanish Parliament which had been elected in 1936, full of enthusiasm and high ideals, had been finally reduced to a bickering rump. The War was lost and the Cortes met here for the last time in February, 1939 before passing over the border into exile, leaving Spain in the hands of Franco.

As I lay down that night in the dungeons of the mediaeval fortress I was completely exhausted by the total unfamiliarity of my life during the last few days. Since breaking away from the carefree pattern of life in Chelsea I had been loaded with a variety of responsibilities which left me with the conviction that I was now totally committed to the situation. It was not only that there was no going back on having joined the army but, what was far more important, that by doing so I had accepted and approved the whole amorality which is part of the condition of militarism. A soldier is not a man who has responsibility to his own concept of right or wrong: he is a unit whose only duty is to obey the orders received, however abhorrent they may appear. This abandonment of personal responsibility horrified me and called for an immensely powerful assurance of the justice of our cause. In a sense, every man is responsible for the killing and other beastlinesses done in his name, and the military situation I was now experiencing was bringing it uncomfortably close to home.

When we woke up on the following morning and emerged from our dungeon, we found it was bright sunshine. There were beautiful views in all directions and walls were bright with pots of geraniums, still in flower. The previous evening we had all been pretty much exhausted after two nights on the train and by the general feeling of insecurity and chaos which had pervaded the fort at Perpignan. Now we had arrived at an official Spanish barracks and all the uncertainty was over. We were able to clean ourselves up and received an excellent breakfast. In fact, we had all been so deeply involved in our own personal problems that we had lost sight of the fact that today was Christmas morning. After a short parade and checking of the nominal roll we were dismissed with permission to go down into the town on leave until midnight. It was Christmas day but there was nothing very Christmasy about the barracks in Figueras. True, it was the most beautiful barracks in Spain. It was clean, the food was tolerable, the building, and its setting in the Pyrenean foothills, was exquisite, but it was still a barracks. In addition it was run by Communists who neither recognized, nor approved of Christmas. We decided to get away down to the town as quickly as possible.

I went off with the Hackney contingent to see what we could find in the way of Christmas fare. The town showed few signs of war, except that there was very little to buy in the shops. Clasp knives and daggers appeared to be the only local products. They came in all sizes and shapes, long, thin, murderous-looking knives, with blades that locked into position to form a dagger. Everybody bought a knife which made us feel very brave and warlike. Apart from the knives, the town had very little to offer except some rather depressing bars and evil-smelling brothels. We all thought that it might be our last chance and it would be a pity to miss it. The whores were very amiable and motherly to us so that our visit was like a twisted family tea-party. They fed us and patted us and told us that we were fine brave kids. They asked us endless questions about our mothers and sisters, what trades we followed and all the intimate details of family life, so that it seemed almost indecent to introduce any erotic element into the proceedings. The gentleness and mothering continued even after we got up from the table and were led off to our separate rooms. The whole situation was more reminiscent of the sick-room of a spoilt child being fussed over by Mummy and Nanny than a sexual extravaganza as a prelude to war.

We were only two days in Figueras before we entrained for Barcelona.

It was still early morning when we marched out of the castle and through the town, and a beautiful sunny day. We sang our songs and carried the red banner, supplied by the Political Commissar of the fort. There were only about sixty of us ragged-looking civilians, but the town turned out in crowds along the sidewalk, making the clenched fist salute and shouting slogans and other forms of encouragement. For the first time we began to feel that we really were rather fine fellows and that the people of Spain did in fact appreciate us. Up to this point I had an unpleasant nag at the back of my mind that maybe I had taken up a rather Quixotic and *Boy's Own Paper* attitude, casting myself in the absurd role of a knight in shining armour going out to defend the oppressed.

The position of a middle-class person in a working-class movement is always anomalous, particularly in such a class-obsessed country as England. It involves an elaborate pattern of pretence on both sides which is embarrassing and absurd. It is ridiculous to pretend that class differences do not exist; above all, in a movement which is primarily concerned with the class struggle. One is constantly embarrassed by the fear of appearing to patronize and of being patronized. But here in Spain one was free of the whole thing. A Spanish working man does not – and cannot – distinguish between one class and another amongst a group of foreigners so that I was able to submerge any difference in the whole pattern of events. It is notable that many middle-class Englishmen went to serve in Spanish units, rather than with groups of their own nationality. John Cornford and George Orwell, for example, both joined the POUM Militia. In Spain I was simply one of an undifferentiated mass, joined together in a common cause to fight and struggle for an ideal that was infinitely larger than any of us. We felt that freedom and justice were indivisible and that a victory over Fascism in Spain was a victory for the whole world, in the sense that we were not merely fighting against a local general's revolt but also against Hitler, Mussolini and all others of the same kind. I was now absolutely certain that I had done the right thing by coming to Spain and was a great deal happier than I had been for some time. Even the train ride to Barcelona in old wooden carriages retained the triumphal air. At every station there were crowds to greet us with food, wine and small bunches of flowers. Banners were waved, clenched fist salutes were exchanged and a variety of slogans chanted. The sun shone and we all felt that we were at the centre of one of the great events of history. The battered old train with its wooden seats rattled along from one station to another in a kind of triumphal progress, all the way across Catalonia.

On our arrival at Barcelona station we were met by a huge reception. Bands were playing on the platform, there were red flags and banners, and the chanting of revolutionary slogans. Here we were, about 250 rather scruffy civilians from a dozen different countries. We could not have presented any sort of military appearance but we were greeted with ecstasy by the enormous crowds that gathered as we proceeded through the city on our way to the artillery barracks. I can't imagine that anyone supposed that we were anything remarkable as a military asset. What value we possessed was purely symbolic. Spain was not to be left alone to fight the monstrous armies of Germany and Italy.

The barracks in which we were billeted for the next three days had been the centre of a battle which had lasted for several weeks. At the outset of the revolt the Commanding General had declared in favour of Franco. The garrison had been besieged by the townspeople with the support of those naval and military units that had remained true to their oath in support of the Republic. It must have been a weird situation, with most of the city living a more or less normal life while a large-scale battle was being fought in the suburbs. The trenches around the barracks had been manned by someone who might have had lunch in the city and then ridden out on the tram to relieve somebody else who had been in the trenches for hours. He, in his turn, would hand over his rifle and catch the tram home to have dinner with his family. The battle had continued until the arrival of miners from Asturias who had blown a breach in the walls which enabled the place to be stormed and overwhelmed. The whole barracks was still in an appalling state of dirt and chaos when we arrived. Nobody seemed to be in charge of the place and crowds of militia-men seemed to come and go as they felt inclined, but everyone was exceedingly amiable. Our draft was given a meal after which we were free to go out on the town.

This was the Barcelona which Orwell describes in *Homage to Catalonia*. It was unmistakably a revolutionary city. The masses had conquered the streets of Barcelona and were now proud in their ownership. All the large public buildings had been taken over by the militia of one party or another, plastered with their banners and posters and guarded by armed men dressed in the *mono* – a blue denim boiler-suit, a khaki forage cap and a red or red and black neckerchief. These militiamen were paid by the political party of which they were members, disposed according to their party's inclination, and maintained in buildings which had been taken over by them. The majority were affiliated to the CNT (*Confederaciōn Nacional del Trabajo*), the Syndicalist Trades Union organized by the Anarchists. Anarchist was a pretty loose term in Spain. It could mean anything from the true doctrinaire Anarchist who believed that there should be no state organization whatsoever, to the Syndicalist who visualized a society in which the Trades Unions appointed delegates from each industry to form a City Council, which in its turn appointed delegates to the Provincial Council and so on, up to the National Council of Labour. The National Council formed not so much a government as a co-ordinating body of all Trades Union activity. The second largest grouping in Barcelona appeared to be the POUM (*Partido Obrero de Unificaciōn Marxista*) which the Communists usually described as Trotskyist. In reality, they had nothing to do with Leon Trotsky, but were a Communist party that did not accept the Moscow line. There was the UGT (*Uniōn General de Trabajadores*) who were roughly equivalent to the English TUC but not affiliated to any political party. Finally the PSUC (*Partido Socialista Unificado de Cataluña*), an uneasy union of Socialists, Communists and Catalan nationalists. Each group participated in the running of the city and the various agricultural areas of Catalonia. And each maintained their separate military units on the Northern Fronts. In reality none of these groups had the doctrinaire political character which has been ascribed to them and they represented nothing more than the various political tendencies of the period. There had been more or less violent fighting all over the city at the outset of the revolt but the majority of people were not dues-paying members of any political organization. The crowds in the street called out, 'Long live the Revolution'. The Communists replied 'Long live the Popular Front' although they well knew that Azaña, the President, and the elected Cortes no longer existed as a viable form of government.

There appeared to be no lack of arms in the city in spite of all that

1. Jason Gurney (on right) in Spain, with Ed Flaherty,
one of the Boston-Irish contingent

2. Civilian troops preparing to defend Madrid in November 1936
   (*Associated Press Photo*)

3. Militiamen commandeer a bus in Barcelona
   (*United Press International*)

we had heard of shortages at the Front. All the sentries on buildings were armed with rifles and there must have been thousands of them. Everyone of any standing wore a Sam Browne belt and carried an automatic pistol, which had already become a status-symbol throughout the Republic. Theoretically, all this armament was kept in the city as protection against a fifth-column rising but it was an open secret that the parties were afraid of one another. In January there was still a pretence of solidarity between the various groups, but as early as May the mutual antipathies broke into open warfare in the streets of Barcelona.

The city was covered in posters and banners carrying political slogans. Collars and ties disappeared and everyone considered it wise to adopt a proletarian form of dress. Hats, other than the militia forage cap, had disappeared. There was practically nothing to buy in the shops, which together with the restaurants had been taken over by the employees and run as co-operatives. The restaurants were reasonably well supplied with everything other than bread. The great grainlands of Spain were nearly all in the area held by Franco and the fighting had started just before harvest time so that bread remained chronically short throughout the War. Farms and factories had also been taken over to be run as co-operatives, and were still distributing wages on the pre-War scale. All these things were the superficialities of Barcelona – what was exciting was the glorious feeling of optimism; the conviction that anything that was not right with society would assuredly be put right in the new world of universal equality and freedom which lay ahead. It may have lacked realism, but it was heady stuff to a young man who was by nature a romantic, and I drank deeply of it. I felt that these men really were my comrades as I had never felt amongst the Communist bureaucrats at home, and I was positively sure that I had done the right thing in coming to Spain to help them in their struggle.

The military revolt had achieved something for the numerous factions of the Left that they had never been able to achieve for themselves: it had united them. True, they were not to remain united for more than a few months, but in January 1937 they were still enjoying the honeymoon period. Everybody was loving everyone else and all were convinced that a glorious future of happiness and prosperity lay ahead of them. The fact that they had been unable to produce a leader of sufficient quality to bind them together into a single force should have been a warning of the future divisions that would destroy the movement. Idealism and rhetoric were not enough. The situation required the formulation of a specific plan of action which would reflect the public will, and a leader who had the capacity to enjoin its acceptance. But in the meanwhile it was a fantastic experience to participate in this apparently universal euphoria of the streets.

Although I was unaware of it at the time, Barcelona held the key to basic flaws which were to destroy the Republic. The political parties at the time of the General's revolt represented only a small minority of the population of Spain. The vast majority were vaguely to the right or left in their political allegiance and the parties on either side of the fence were hopelessly divided one against the other. The two Royalist parties were bitterly opposed to one another, as were the two Fascist parties. The centre parties were little more than talking shops for the intelligentsia. The left-wing parties were bitterly divided between the Socialist factions and the Anarchists. The revolt forced all the parties of the right into the arms of General Franco. But the left-wing elements tended to coalesce around the more extreme elements of the left movement, because they were the most energetic and dynamic political forces. The immediate result of this situation was that the effective leadership of the Popular Front passed into the hands of the revolutionary element. Largo Caballero, head of the non-Anarchist section of the Trades Union movement with its one and a half million members, suddenly realized the mood of the time and switched from a political position of support for workers' control and active participation in the workers' syndicates which took over the running of industry and agriculture in most cities, and even in village communes. Every political faction was trying to outdo the others in revolutionary zeal and to gain control of the popular movement. By an extraordinary paradox the one political party which was opposed to the revolutionary trend was the Stalinist section of the Communist Party.

The Comintern foreign policy at this time was to submerge the Communist Parties of all the capitalist countries into an alliance with all the parties left of centre, to create a mildly left-wing coalition which would support an alliance with the USSR. The Communist Parties were instructed to cut out all reference to revolutionary matter from their propaganda and move into a purely reformist stance; the Party was to become sufficiently respectable to attract the radical members of the middle classes and thus become a more effective instrument in each country in support of Russian policies. This was pretty hard for the diehard revolutionaries to take but was justified as being a necessary tactic in defence of the USSR against the rising tide of Fascism in Europe. From a purely Russian standpoint this was a perfectly logical and reasonable attitude but it was disastrous for the prosecution of the War against Franco in Spain.

It was the revolutionary elements in Spain that had gone out on the streets in the early days of the revolt to defend the Republic. They had defeated the regular Army in pitched battles all over the peninsula in every major city bar five, in spite of their lack of arms or organization. And it was no more than a dream that the petty bourgeois clerks and shopkeepers would join them to fight against the Army and the Church. The Stalinist section of the Communist Party was the smallest political party in Spain but they possessed a number of outstanding advantages. They were extremely well disciplined and highly organized. In a country like Spain, this gave them a tremendous advantage over all their opponents. Their principal strength was in the capital where they soon gained control of the situation and thus controlled the central Government. They exploited every situation with exceptional courage and brilliance in support of a policy diametrically opposed to the masses to whom they were supposedly allied. They alone had a world-wide organization to support them with propaganda and money; their ultimate sanction lay in the fact that they could always count on a supply of the materials of war from the USSR.

In January the cities were effectually ruled by Committees which were controlled by more or less revolutionary groups, usually Anarchist or left-wing Socialist of one complexion or another. It was only in Madrid that the Communists had effective control. Barcelona was principally under the control of the Anarchists, POUM and the extreme left-wing regionalists who wanted an independent Catalonia. The POUM was a uniquely Spanish organization. It was a Marxist-Communist Party but was entirely Spanish-controlled and accepted no directives from Russia or anywhere else. The Russian Communists described its members as Trotskyists and hated them more bitterly than anyone in Spain – the orthodox loathing for the heretic and, like the religions of old, the heretic was infinitely more abominable than the heathen. This party had very little membership outside Barcelona and soon became isolated, but in January it was one of the most important parties in the city and supported a considerable militia on the Northern Front.

Barcelona is always a fascinating and wonderful city but under the present circumstances I found it deliriously exciting. Everybody that I met was kind and helpful. I ate and drank and made hundreds of undying friendships with people I have never met since. My only disappointment was that I was unable to get in to visit the interior of the Sagrada Familia Cathedral which I had wanted to see for years. In a city where everything else was going flat out, only the churches and other religious establishments were closed. The streets were crowded with people at all hours of the day and night. Crowds of men and women thronged the Ramblas, and on Parallelo all the bars, brothels and honky-tonk shows were in full blast throughout the twenty-four hours of the day. There were processions, with or without military bands, flags everywhere, the singing of all kinds of revolutionary songs, and the chanting of slogans. Every political group was trying to outdo its rivals with political posters and the whole city was a riot of colour and sound.

After two days amongst the flesh-pots of Barcelona we were organized into another procession down to the station. There were more bands, more banners, and more cheering crowds. We spent another night on the bare, wooden benches of a third-class carriage and woke up on the following morning as the train was running through the suburbs of Valencia. Again we were met with bands and banners and marched around the town, but here the situation was totally different from that which we had experienced in Barcelona. The Valencians seemed almost indifferent to the political situation and there was very little sign of popular activity. Personally, I began to feel that we were being used for a propaganda stunt which I resented. In any case we were all dead-tired and bored with marching around: there was little response in the streets and the whole affair was pretty much of a flop. Finally, we were glad to climb aboard another third-class carriage for another miserable night journey to Albacete which had become the centre for the International Brigades. Here we were herded into a large and gloomy barracks which had previously been occupied by the Guardia Civil—the sinister para-military police force with varnished black hats, which had become a symbol of oppression throughout the country. We marched through a stone tunnel, with the guardroom on one side of it, into a courtyard. This establishment was ruled by a tall, good-looking Frenchman known as Vidal, who came out to inspect us accompanied by a dozen of his villainous looking henchmen, all heavily armed. This unsavoury crew ran the barracks as they felt inclined, without any apparent control from the higher command. They lived in the guardhouse where they loafed around like a bunch of gangsters, with great pistols on their hips. They spread themselves over the guardroom with drinks in their hands and their feet on the desks, without any pretence at military discipline or any serious attempt to see that the barracks were properly maintained. There was a constant flow of new recruits and men on their way from hospital, either to return to their units or to be repatriated. Nobody stayed long enough to interest themselves in the affairs of the barracks and the whole system was wide open to abuse. When we were issued with our uniform we were obliged to hand over our civilian clothing and all our personal effects. As far as I know, none of it was ever returned – certainly when I was invalided out I asked for my suitcase but got no satisfaction. Nobody received any mail or cigarette ration. The food was exceedingly poor and there was very little of it. Eventually Vidal and his gang were brought to book after nearly twelve months during which time they must have pillaged about 20,000 volunteers.

After breakfast on the following morning we were all marched down to the city bull ring and paraded according to national groups. There must have been about 600 men of all nationalities. The largest contingents were French and German; the British contingent had now increased to about sixty, by the addition of various extras, including one American, one Abyssinian – reputed to be the son of a general, a refugee from Mussolini's occupation of his country – and half-a-dozen Cypriots, who had all asked to join up with us as they spoke English and had no national group of their own. In the centre of the bull ring there was a table with a number of uniformed officers standing around. Eventually, one of them came out in front and explained in French that we were to be allocated to the units in which we would serve. First he called for anyone who had served in the artillery or cavalry. Then electricians, telephonists and motor mechanics. It was typical of the English that after a hurried colloquy we decided that we would all sooner stay together and go into the poor bloody infantry, rather than get mixed up with a lot of foreigners. So none of our lot professed any special skills or volunteered for anything. It took hours to sort out the various individuals who proposed themselves as there were at least fifteen different language groups. A tremendous amount of arguing and expostulation seemed to be going on around the table, but we solemnly stood at ease until we were marched back to the barracks for lunch, and a pretty stupid looking bunch we must have seemed, without a single military skill amongst the lot of us.

After the sorting-out process was complete we were treated to a harangue by André Marty, the chief Political Commissar of the International Brigades. He had first made his name as the leader of a naval mutiny in the Black Sea. The French Navy had been sent out to aid the White Russian forces against the Reds, but the sailors had refused to fight and conducted a successful mutiny. André Marty, who had of course been thrown out of the French Navy for his part in the mutiny, had joined the Communist Party and risen to be a member of the Central Committee. He may have been a great chap in his day, but in Spain he was both a sinister and a ludicrous figure. He was a large, fat man with a bushy moustache, and always wore a huge, black beret – looking like a caricature of an old-fashioned French petty bourgeois. There is no doubt that he was quite literally mad at this time. He always spoke in an hysterical roar, he suspected everyone of treason, or worse, listened to advice from nobody, ordered executions on little or no pretext – in short he was a real menace. Later he admitted to the execution of 500 men belonging to the International Brigades, but this is generally agreed to have been a very conservative estimate. He now stood yelling away at us in French, which the majority of those present did not understand. It was a fantastic polemic which seemed to make very little sense and did nothing to encourage a bunch of very raw recruits in a strange country.

On our return to barracks we were ordered into a storeroom to receive our uniforms. Nobody was in charge of the job and the various items just lay in heaps around the store. Each man foraged for whatever fitted him best. No importance was attached to uniform in the Republic, and most of my fellows had to make do with a thin, cotton corduroy jacket, buttoning at the neck, and trousers of the same material which were painfully inadequate in the cold weather of the Sierra. They were of various shades of brown, and the jacket and trousers seldom matched, but it was the nearest thing to uniformity there was. I am usually very lucky or very unlucky with issue clothing, owing to my unusual size, but on this occasion I was superbly fortunate in finding a thick, woollen, khaki ski-suit. The standard issue of boots had nothing in my size but I finally discovered a pair made of chrome leather which served me well right up until I was wounded. We were all topped off with a khaki beret and began to assume some sort of military appearance. Poor Tiny Silverman had been through every garment in the place without finding anything to fit him except a beret.

We each received two thin, cotton blankets, rolled into a sausage-like arrangement with the two ends tied together and worn like a bandolier. Then there was the groundsheet cape which seems to be an inevitable part of the equipment of every British soldier. This depressing piece of rubberized cloth with the four corners flapping about at uneven lengths reduces even the smartest group of soldiers to the appearance of a rabble. Undoubtedly it is a very useful garment, but there is no possible means of wearing it without looking like a moth-eaten bird with a broken wing. Next came the leather equipment – a belt with a brass buckle, cross straps, a bayonet frog and two large ammunition boxes attached to the front of it. This proved a most inconvenient arrangement as the cartridge boxes were so large that they seemed to get in the way every time we moved. Finally we received a tin-helmet of a French army pattern, 1918 War vintage. In spite of its dashing appearance, it was made of very thin metal and was quite useless as a protection against anything more lethal than kids throwing stones.

We were now fully kitted out as soldiers and practically unable to move. All that we lacked were rifles and bayonets, but we did not acquire these until the very last day before going up to the Front. We had given up our personal identities when we had surrendered our personal property and accepted the army uniform, and were now authentic soldiers of the Spanish Republic. An order had been issued that everybody should hand in their passports or other documents of identity. This, I felt, was going too far. I had knocked about in too many places where the going was hard not to realize the importance of being able to prove who you are and where you come from in moments of real emergency. So I just kept quiet and hid my passport away in the inner pocket of my uniform jacket. I did not mind becoming a soldier, but saw no reason to abandon my individual identity.

Albacete must have been a dreary provincial town at the best of times. Most of the streets and sidewalks had broken paving or none at all. Before the War it had been the market town and administrative centre of an exceedingly poor agricultural district. There were no buildings of any distinction, and those that existed bore very obvious signs of neglect. There was a small central square with half-a-dozen ragged palms and a small park that looked as if no one had ever taken any real interest in it. A large, old-fashioned hotel which had previously provided accommodation for commercial travellers and visiting business men had now been taken over by the nabobs of the International Brigades. Most of them were dressed in the most extraordinary collection of self-invented uniforms – leather coats in many lengths and colours, breeches with an assortment of spectacular-looking highboots of all kinds, and a beret. They all wore Sam Browne belts of varying and elaborate design, with large, business-like pistols. No one would forgo this last status symbol, although they were useless in the city and urgently needed at the Front.

There appeared to be no Spanish troops or police around the town, and very few townspeople. The rain drizzled down continuously on the muddy streets and the whole place was as depressing as only a Spanish provincial town can be on a wet day. The only places of recreation were the International Brigades Club and a rather pretentious café. The club consisted of a large hall, two continental-type billiard tables, chairs, tables and a bar. Here it was interesting to watch the behaviour of the various national groups. The Germans delighted to sit around in a large circle singing revolutionary songs with all the precision of a steam organ. There were only about eight of these songs and they repeated the repertoire over and over again, from opening time until they were thrown out at night. There was never any variation in the singing of a particular song and no individual peculiarities were permitted. The effect was exceedingly monotonous but it appeared to give them some sort of peculiarly Teutonic satisfaction. The French drank and played billiards, and indulged in all kinds of animated argument while wreathed in clouds of tobacco smoke. The English drank and complained. They didn't like the place or the people, they hated the grub and they thought the beer was lousy – the peculiarly English way of expressing home-sickness. The café was quite an elegant affair with a modern shopfront and fittings which must have been reconstructed just before the War. It offered the oddest selection of luxuries – expresso coffee, thin slices of Dutch cheese, little bottles of sweet vermouth and nothing else.

The most exciting thing in town was the man who sold roast potatoes in the square. They were roasted in their jackets and slit open on one side to receive a little salt and olive oil. They were always magnificently hot and provided us with the only palatable food we could find. We were all delighted when the order came for us to pack up and be ready to join the Battalion.

4

Madrigueras — The Burrows

In the afternoon a couple of trucks came to pick us up for the journey to the village of Madrigueras, where the British Battalion training depot had been established. After only about an hour's drive through the drizzling rain we pulled up outside the one substantial-looking building in a very dull and depressing village. This, the driver announced, was our Battalion Headquarters.

Even the name of the place was pathetic – Madrigueras: the Burrows. It had never been much of a village – out in the middle of the bare, featureless plain of Murcia where even an occasional tree is a thing of wonder. The whole region had been farmed by absentee landlords, so that the population had been herded into the smallest available area in order not to encroach on any part of the productive land. This system produces a very gloomy landscape, with no dwellings between one village and the next. Everywhere lay under a chill and drizzling rain, and in Madrigueras itself the unpaved streets had become churned up into a grey-green mud which got thicker and soupier with every passing day. There was no fuel for heating and everyone in the village lived in a permanent condition of damp clothes and damp houses, breathing in the awful moisture-sodden air. Maybe it was a nice enough place in summer but now, in January, it was unbearably depressing. The poverty of the local population was really frightening. Their principal dish seemed to be cold, boiled potatoes sliced up into a six-inch frying pan with oil and garlic and a beaten egg to bind it together, cooked over a fire made from pieces of last year's vine-prunings chopped into half-a-dozen, four-inch lengths a pencil thick. And on this diet, with bread and wine, they appeared to subsist.

They were a silent and taciturn people who looked as if they had given up hope. I was fortunate in being able to speak a certain amount of Spanish and was one of the very few British people who could communicate with them. As far as I could ever discover they did not approve or disapprove of our presence in the village. They were always civil in a rather grave and solemn way, but they appeared to have no strong political feelings at all. The UGT had come into the village and set up the Casa del Pueblo which existed in every village as a political and social centre. It was decorated with the usual vivid posters and had a bar selling coffee, anis and grappa, but very few people used the place – three or four groups of silent men in shabby clothes with black hats and black scarves wrapped around the lower part of their faces. The women walked around the town with black shawls over their heads. They, too, were solemn and polite if spoken to, but all the life seemed to have gone out of them. It was now winter in a despoiled and empty world. There was neither warmth nor heat nor light nor food nor health nor love, and the village population stayed on through sheer inertia. Their only source of hope lay in their treasure – the saddest, most pathetic treasure in all of time – a neat cubic bale measuring only about twenty-four inches in each dimension. And this pathetic little package kept a whole village tied. They knew it was worth a fortune. They did not know where to sell it or what to do with it, but it represented such an ecstasy of work and suffering that they could not bear to leave it. It stood locked in a little room, on a stand like an altar – the life, the soul, and the suffering of a poverty-stricken village. The cold, grey fields around the village were planted with unending rows of little bulbs, as regular and as closely-set as wheatlands. Crocuses, millions and millions of crocus bulbs. Crocuses which would bloom again in the next springtime, from which the few hundred peasants of Madrigueras would pluck the stamens – ten thousand to the ounce – to be dried in the sun to produce saffron, and another of those pathetic bales. The hopes, the sufferings and the fears of a whole village – a whole world.

The village church showed evidence of the violent desecration which seemed to have been general all over the country. It was a very large building for such a small village, with a tower tall enough to be seen for miles across the plain. The high altar, the pews, and all signs of religious painting had been removed. The sculptures had been defaced like those one sees in English churches which were subject to violence at the time of the Reformation. When we arrived in the village the Church had already been converted into a Battalion mess-hall – the field-kitchens occupying the chancel area, and tables with benches in the nave. I never saw any village people enter it and they even seemed to avoid looking at the place, as if they had a sense of guilt about it. I never discovered what had actually happened there, but it left me with an uneasy feeling that something had occurred which everybody preferred to forget.

The whole business of the desecration of the churches in Spain remains for me one of the greatest mysteries of the Civil War period. At no time or place in history has there been such a violence of hatred against a national religion. There was no bestiality that was not committed upon the persons of priests, and occasionally of nuns, who were the only women to be consistently mistreated in the Republican areas. These were not isolated incidents, nor were they restricted to political fanatics. In every village that I saw the churches had been destroyed or desecrated with an extreme of hatred and detestation that was unmistakable and everything that I was able to find out about events led me to the conviction that very few people in any village had not actively participated in the revulsion. There must have been a reason for it all. A great many people abandon the Church of their fathers but few of them feel any violence against it. In Spain, the degree of violence, and the universality of it, cannot be doubted. In talking to village people in many places, the principal charge to be made against the clergy was of practising hypocrisy in many forms – chiefly of deceiving the poor for the benefit of the rich, as is common both in France and in Italy where it is regarded with a more or less cynical tolerance. But in Spain the Church appeared to be totally identified with every kind of suffering and oppression. It had become the scapegoat for every sin of omission or commission by the ruling caste. The villagers frequently had never seen the landlord whose activities left them in such desperate poverty but they felt that the Church was his friend and the Church had enjoined them to suffer their poverty without protest – the Church was their enemy. The princes of the Church were the habitual companions of the princes of the land – the Church was their enemy. The Church was the friend of the Police and Guardia Civil – the Church was their enemy. The price which the Church had paid was frightening. There is no excuse for the appalling atrocities which undoubtedly occurred all over Spain but there must have been a reason – and whether the reasons have now been examined and corrected, I doubt.

We climbed out of the trucks on the drizzling morning of our arrival in the village and fell in as smartly as we knew how. Since we had not been allowed to take any personal baggage with us when we left Albacete, we had now arrived with nothing but the clothes we stood up in, and must have seemed a sorry-looking bunch, standing in the rain in our sloppy rig, with the leather harness and blanket roll worn diagonally over the top. Under these circumstances it was impossible to present any sort of martial appearance and we felt like fools. Our reception was something less than enthusiastic. A motley-looking half-dozen emerged from the Headquarters building and strolled around us in a desultory sort of way. This was the Battalion HQ staff, and a strange assortment they turned out to be.

Wilfred Macartney was in command of the Battalion. He was a strange man whom I came to know quite well several years later. At this time he had recently been released from Parkhurst Prison where he had served a ten years' sentence, having been convicted of spying for the USSR. The book of his prison experience, *Walls Have Mouths*, published by the Left Book Club, was enjoying a considerable vogue. He was a rich and well-educated man, a great drinker and bon viveur, and I find it difficult to believe he was ever a very dedicated Communist. In any case, it soon became evident that he had very little idea of the duties of a Battalion Commander.

Apart from his appearance at the morning parade, he appeared to leave the running of the Battalion to his Adjutant and to the Political Commissar, Dave Springhall, a pleasant, but hopelessly obtuse and humourless man. He was later imprisoned in England for spying on behalf of the Nazis. I never discovered what caused the switch in his allegiance, and he was the last person in the world that I should ever have expected to change sides. His principal function at Madrigueras seemed to be the delivery of exceedingly boring homilies at the morning parades which were always prefaced with the phrase, 'Now comrades, the position is as follows.' He seemed to be a well-intentioned man who was completely out of his depth in the position in which he found himself.

The function of a Political Commissar at its best is very similar to that of a Chaplain in the British Army. His first job is welfare. He serves as a buffer between officers and soldiers, and functions as the source of moral authority. He endeavours to fulfil these tasks without possessing any kind of power. He cannot give orders but must operate entirely by virtue of persuasion. That is the theory: in practice he may be something approaching a Secret Police spy, of whom everyone is terrified. He frequently falls somewhere between the two, but he can only be as good as the people who appoint him. The nearest thing to a good Political Commissar that I saw was George Aitkin, who took over that function in the British Battalion at Jarama. He was a Scots Communist about forty years of age, strong in his Communist convictions but by no means uncritical. If he thought that the leadership was wrong he did not hesitate to say so, with the result that he was eventually sent home and resigned from the Party.

Tom Wintringham, once of Balliol College, Oxford, and more recently war correspondent of the *Daily Worker*, was Second in Command. Wintringham is frequently quoted as being the originator of the whole idea of the International Brigades but this I think is very improbable as he was never sufficiently important in the hierarchy to have been in a position to influence Party policy. There has been endless nonsense written about who invented the International Brigades. But the whole point is that nobody invented them at all. From the very day of the rising, all sorts of individuals set out for Spain to assist the embattled Republic. It immediately appeared as the symbol of a great number of things which men held valuable but which were being destroyed all over Europe. To the Italian and German refugees, it was an opportunity to fight against the dictators who had destroyed their homeland; to the Greeks, the military who had been corroding democracy in their country; to the various Balkan peoples, it was a symbol of resistance against the variety of oppressive regimes at home; to the British and French, a chance to protest against the hopelessly corrupt and inefficient ruling cliques who were leading them into another world war or an accommodation with Hitler. The Communists had the good sense to realize the terrific force of idealism that existed and climbed on the band-wagon to exploit it. Huge sums of money were collected, their campaigns were supported by the famous and the influential, their rallies and demonstrations were attended by thousands. They possessed an international organization and understood the techniques of propaganda, with the result that at no time in history have they received more popular support in England and France, even in America, than at the time they gave their backing to the International Brigades.

Wintringham was at this time a slim man of medium height, with large, round, steel-framed spectacles, a high-domed bald head and an academic stoop, about thirty-five years old. He always wore a khaki beret, a shiny black mackintosh coat of a vaguely military cut, riding breeches and high laced boots. The total effect suggested a motorcyclist rather than a soldier. He was invariably pleasant, informal and unpretentious. I don't think that he really knew any more about military affairs than I did, but he was a completely sincere radical who did his best to be useful to the cause without any idea of personal aggrandizement. His only apparent vice was a weakness for delivering long and rather tedious lectures on the Marxist theory of warfare. In spite of lack of practical experience of soldiering, he was an indefatigable military theorist. One of his obsessions was the similarity he imagined to exist between our War and the American Civil War, on the basis of which he evolved a whole pattern of theories as to how our War must inevitably progress and of the strategies and techniques which we should employ. The lectures were heavily larded with texts from Marx and Engels which were supposed to reinforce the argument. Perhaps the theory might have had greater validity if we had possessed an Abraham Lincoln. As it was, Spain was totally lacking in any political figure who could bring cohesion or unity into the Republican cause.

The real *eminence gris* of the Communist Party in Madrigueras was Peter Kerrigan who remains to this day one of the senior members of the British Communist Party, one of the very few who have ridden every 'crisis of conscience' which has beset the Party – the excesses of Stalin, the Second World War, the conquest of the satellite countries, to the recent invasion of Czechoslovakia. As I remember him in Madrigueras, he was a tall, well-built man with a thick poll of tightly crinkled hair, as dour and ill-tempered as only a Scot can be, utterly devoid of any trace of humour and with a total acceptance of the Party line. Calvin would have loved him. He wore some sort of semi-military costume and a large, practical-looking automatic pistol. He was always present on every official occasion but never made any public utterance.

The smallest man on the Battalion HQ staff was MacDade, who claimed to be Irish and one of the heroes of the Easter Rising. He said he had been a sergeant-major in the Irish Guards – although he was only a couple of inches above five foot tall. He was a prodigious liar and a natural clown but he had evidently been in the British Army somewhere and at some time, as he was a master of parade ground and orderly room punctilio, on the basis of which Macartney had appointed him Battalion Adjutant. Whether he had any knowledge of the practical arts of war I never discovered as I never saw him again after he went up to the Front. His personal appearance was no great asset to his military pretensions as he was very small, with a round, pink face and straight, blond hair and wore large, round spectacles.

Theoretically the Battalion organization consisted of the Battalion Commander, his Second in Command, the Political Commissar, the Adjutant and orderly room staff, three Companies of infantry, one machine-gun Company, Battalion scouts and the Quarter-master and cookhouse staff. There were three platoons in each Company, divided into sections of ten men, so that the Battalion at full strength would number more than 500 men. The first Battalion that went up to Jarama was somewhere above this number. Nearly 400 were lost in the first two days of the battle and it never again rose to full strength. The officers at Company and Platoon level were Communist Party members who had shown capacity for organization and leadership in the political world at home. Unfortunately none of them had any real knowledge or experience of military affairs. They were all exceedingly conscientious and did their very best in a completely unfamiliar situation, but good intentions were a poor substitute for technical skill. Party meetings were held at all levels from time to time and the organization permeated every level of activity.

The root of the whole situation lay in the command's ambivalent attitude towards discipline. This was a people's army and everybody was addressed as Comrade and referred to by function – Comrade Battalion Command, Comrade Political Commissar, down to just Comrade. We were all supposed to be equal in some respects but not in others and just where the division lay was always obscure. The confusion between

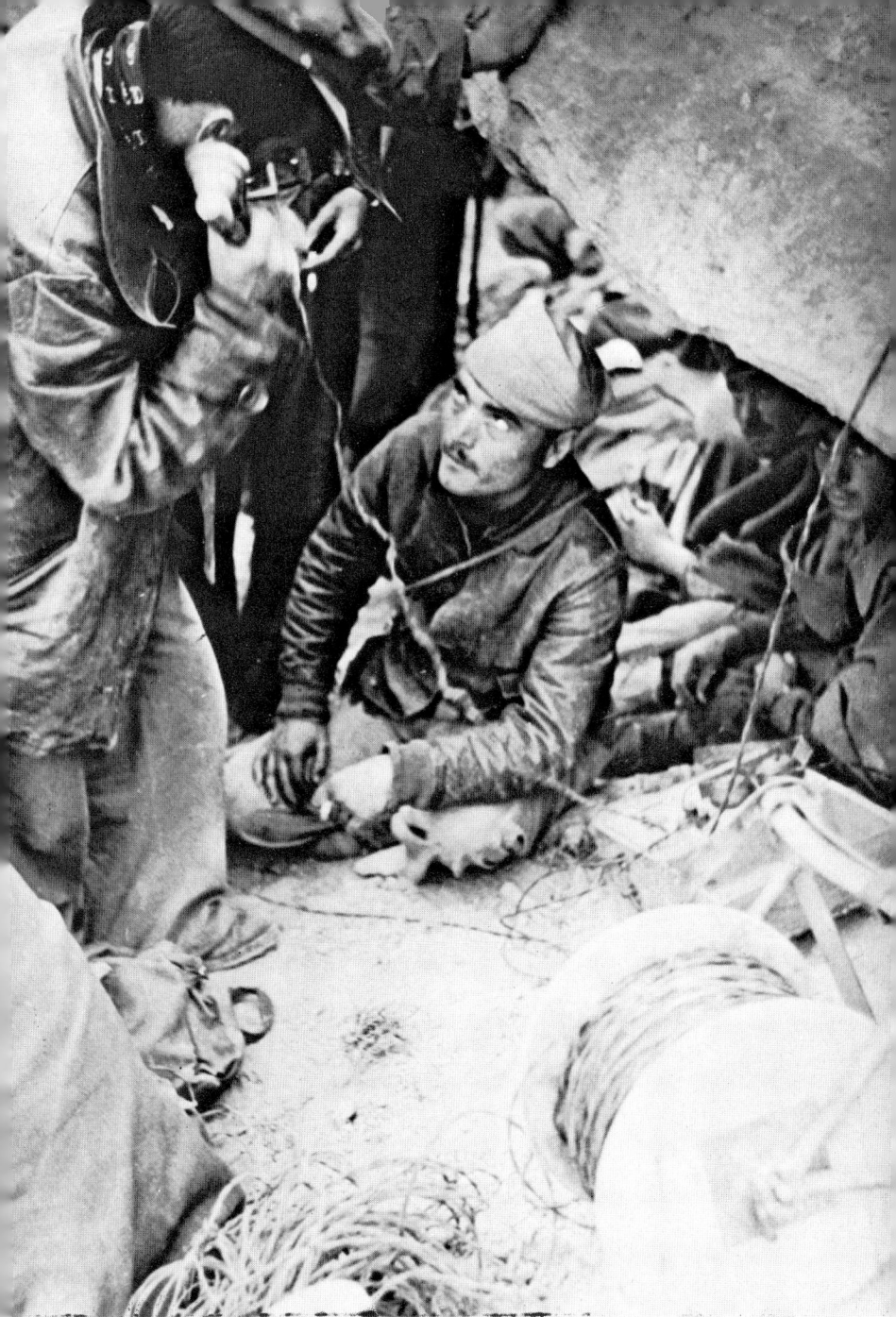

4. Communications in the front line *(Robert Capa)*

5. Infantry in action *(Robert Capa)*

6. Artillery bombardment *(United Press International)*

political and military functions or responsibilities was never entirely resolved throughout the history of the International Brigades. This gave rise to a considerable amount of arrant hypocrisy which only the strongest stomach could digest. The Battalion was called the Saklatavala Battalion, later changed to the Clement Attlee from motives of political expediency, in spite of the obvious fact that all the Communists hated Attlee whom they regarded as an enemy of the working class. A typical example of the 'comrade' hypocrisy is illustrated by the occasion when two dishevelled figures arrived at the Battalion HQ. They had obviously been engaged in a fight and the less severely damaged of the pair was dragging along his badly-battered opponent shouting 'This comrade has stolen my watch.'

Macartney and his staff lived in the only decent house in the village which was popularly believed to be the scene of wild luxury and indulgence, contrasting strongly with the life of the rank and file in their squalid billets. No provision had been made for baths or laundry, nor even for the most elementary form of personal ablution. The few lavatories which existed were hopelessly inadequate for the numbers that they had to serve, with the result that the stink in the billets was really abominable. There was plenty of food, but no proper supervision of the cooking arrangements which were dirty and inefficient. The command had made the classical error of military minds by putting all the 'duds' into the cookhouse: the lazy, the incompetent and the dishonest. None of them knew how to cook any dish other than a 'stew' which recurred day after day, varied only by whatever vegetables were available – everything was simply hurled into great cauldrons of water and boiled. While in Madrigueras we had an adequate supply of good bread, made in the local bakery, but when the Battalion moved up to the Front we suffered badly. Bread was always scarce and usually stale, as none of our cooks knew how to bake and we were dependent on whatever supplies could be had from village bakeries around the area.

The billet we were allocated consisted of a cement-floored hall which had once been used as a cinema but now looked more like a disused garage. There wasn't a chair or table or any other piece of furniture in the whole place, and only two wash-basins and two lavatories. We were the first arrivals and in the beginning when there were only twenty of us, it was quite tolerable. Later, when the place housed one hundred men, it became unspeakably disgusting. We were each given two planks and cross battens, a straw palliasse and a pillow, laid on the bare cement floor. Everything was extremely damp, and January on the plains of central Spain is very cold and miserable indeed.

The rank and file of the Battalion were a peculiar kind of mixed bag, drawn from all classes of society. There were pure idealists, political opportunists, doctrinaire Marxists, adventurers and plain rogues, in varying proportions. But the one sure thing was that practically none of them had come to Spain for the reasons they stated. It is strange how a man will invent motives, totally different from his true ones, to account for any serious decision he may take – it is almost as though he were afraid to look at his own image in a mirror. Sometimes life seems like a mad daydream in which a man can never do what he wants to do, but can only invent reasons for behaving as his nature compels him to behave. Here were 600 men living in the shadow of death – 400 of them were to be dead within the next three months – and yet each seemed to be playing out his own private charade as if all reality had passed away. The idealists, submerged in a cloud-cuckoo land of their own imagining, became immune from everyday events. The political opportunists were scuttling around, busily trying to establish a position which most of them never lived to enjoy. The doctrinaire Marxists constantly reassured themselves that they knew exactly what would happen next, like a bunch of political clairvoyants. The adventurers seemed sometimes like the only sane people around – they realized that if they were going to make anything out of this racket they had to be 'good'. So they set about the business of soldiering in a realistic and serious way, determined to come to the top and to survive, which is probably the best set of aspirations for a soldier to have. The rogues were busy after 'bint and booze', and the hell with tomorrow. The majority of us merely hoped that we should not show up too badly when the time came and would be able to justify our existence.

There was a small coterie of middle-class intellectuals who grouped themselves around Giles Romilly, attracted by the glamour of his being a nephew of Winston Churchill. Giles himself was at that time a very pleasant, light-hearted and unpretentious character who, I always felt, had come to Spain out of a spirit of bravado rather than from any deep political conviction. There were about twenty of them in this set and the majority of them were homosexuals. Several were freshly down from the University and they all derived from one or other of the left-intellectual worlds of London. These were amongst the strangest phenomena of the period and existed on no other basis than pure fashion. It had seemed to me absurd that such elegant aesthetes as Herbert Read, Stephen Spender, Auden and Isherwood should go through all the motions of neo-Communism – I had been to a great number of elegant apartments full of charming and highly-educated young men, drinking cocktails and discussing the gossip and minutiae of Communist Party affairs. They talked of the activities of the workers with tremendous intimacy, as if they themselves were personally involved in them. They were regular subscribers to the Left Book Club and the *New Statesman* and used Marxist tracts as coffee-table books. They discussed 'The Revolution' as though they were intimately involved in a conspiracy in which they would burst out with sword and gun onto the streets of London at any minute. It was all very romantic and totally unreal. A few of them had overdone the thing and come to Spain in a spirit of bravado or exhibitionism. The story of Tony Hyndman, alias Johnny Younger, was typical: a member of Stephen Spender's set who came to Spain and hated it, deserted, was captured and held in prison until rescued by his protector. But amongst these groups there were the serious and dedicated Marxists who became important and valuable operatives of the international Communist organization.

One of the puzzling aspects of the Spanish Civil War was the extraordinary fascination which it had for the rich, homosexual aesthetes, particularly in England, of whom Malcolm Dunbar was a classic and even tragic example. In 1936 he was recently down from Trinity College, Cambridge, where he was reputed to have been the leader of an advanced aesthetic set. I came to know him, around the drinking clubs of Chelsea, as a very elegant and evidently rich member of the local intelligentsia. He moved in a totally different world from my own and I never thought of him except as an amusing, if somewhat cynical, character with whom to have a drink. The day before I left England he had apparently heard that I had arranged to go to Spain, and he finally ran me down in the old Studio Club over Harris's chemist shop in the King's Road in order to ask how he should set about joining the International Brigades. It was just before Christmas and the place was full of people celebrating. I was sharing farewell drinks with all and sundry and I did not take him very seriously, but gave him the information that he wanted and went on my way. I was consequently amazed when I ran into him in Madrigueras a couple of weeks later. But the Malcolm in Spain was totally different to the one I had known in the King's Road. He appeared to go out of his way to avoid the upper-class homosexual set and had become intensely serious-minded, if still rather cynical in his attitude to life in general. He took his military duties very seriously and rigorously supported the Party line on everything to do with Spain and the army. It sounded very strange to hear the King's Road Malcolm ranting on about the necessity for organization and discipline. He was wounded at Jarama and went on to the newly-formed Officers' School when he came out of hospital. I never saw him again, but he fought in all the subsequent battles and was Chief of Staff of the XVth Brigade from the last battles on the Ebro until the International Brigades were disbanded in 1938. The end of the War left him apparently without any real purpose in life and he drifted down hill to what appears to have been suicide. He was the only one of his crowd who made a successful – or even enthusiastic – soldier. The majority of them became rather pathetic in their complete inability to live up to the situation in which they had landed themselves.

So much has been written on the subject of the War as it affected the middle classes in England and the number of middle-class individuals that took part in it that the role of the working class gradually became eclipsed. In reality the British working class felt an extreme hatred and fear of Fascism, and they had good reason to do so. They had seen the Trades Unions and every kind of working-class organization destroyed in Germany and Italy. The leaders were all dead or imprisoned, and they themselves were suffering all the miseries of unemployment and the means test. Even the employed were so badly paid that many of them lived barely above the subsistence level.

In Spain they had seen a Popular Front government duly elected, to be immediately overthrown by a *coup d'état* of the ruling class, and they were alive to the fact that it could happen at home. They had reason to fear and to hate Fascism, not merely as individuals of tender conscience, but as an entire class. In the circumstances, it is not remarkable that the overwhelming majority of soldiers in the International Brigades were members of the working class. The constant use of phrases like 'the platoon of poets' creates an entirely false picture. The middle-class intellectuals amongst the 600-strong Battalion in Madrigueras could not by any stretch of the imagination have exceeded thirty, and very few of them turned out to be of any value from a purely military point of view. In the Lincoln (American) Battalion the proportion of intellectuals was considerably higher, but the vast majority of them were strictly and militantly working class. The myth of an army of middle-class writers and poets has arisen from the obvious fact that these were the most vocal section of the organization and that their work forms the easiest form of source material for writers of a later generation. In fact, if we take the entire output on the subject of the Brigades, written by men who served in them, we are left with a very thin corpus and one that can claim little outstanding literary merit or very close attachment to the facts.

One of the most amusing characters in Madrigueras was an ex-Anglican parson, the Reverend R. M. Hilliard, who had become a Communist and had developed the most startlingly irreverent manner by the time I knew him. When in wine he would put on his parsonical voice and make a benediction – 'In the name of Marx,' – and with two fingers raised he made the curve of the sickle. 'Engels' – he drew the handle. 'Lenin, Stalin, Stakinov, Dimitrov' – the points of the hammerhead; 'the Party line' – its handle. All delivered with extreme unction. He was a great drinker and his friends were of all classes. They liked him for his sense of humour and his consistently cheerful attitude.

One old man of whom I became exceedingly fond was Jack Lemaans. Jack was all of a piece. Born in Holland, he had drifted to the States as a kid and had become an Anarchist and spent his life as an active revolutionary in the American Wobblies. He'd been beaten up and jailed in more than half the states of the Union, but neither pain nor hunger and cold had weakened his unalterable faith.

'While there is a working class, I am of it. While there is a revolutionary party, I belong to it, and while there is one man in jail, I am not free.'

'Who said that?' I asked.

'Eugene Debs and I reckon that's all any man wants to know. If we want a decent world of social justice we gotta fight and that's all there is to it. These talking bastards betray the working class every time.'

'But what'll you ever get out of it?'

'I dunno. I guess it's just the way I am. It makes me sick to see people getting kicked around and I get to feel that I got to do something about it.'

'But, Jack, it's got to be more than that. You've got to fight for something.'

'If some bastard's kickin' you in the teeth do you have to stop and ask him what for? Look, that's how the world is – it's the system. One bunch of guys 'ave got the boots and the others get kicked. Until you can wipe out the system it'll go on like that. The rest is all bluff and bullshit. We got to bust the system – bust it wide open and start again and the only way to do that is to fight.'

When the Civil War started he had been in Holland and scorned to be transported to Spain with 'pennies collected from the working class', so he had walked it. About sixty-years old, he was shot through the chest and invalided out a few months later. After he came out of hospital he still refused to be shipped back by train to Holland and set out on foot. His ideas may have been naive but he was a man of absolutely blinding sincerity and I often spent the evenings with him listening to stories of the Wobblies – the International Workers of the World – and their attempt to make an Anarchist revolution in the United States. They believed in sabotage as an instrument of policy, and a large part of Jack's reminiscences were stories of bombing, incendiarism and other deeds of violence. But Jack himself was one of the kindest, gentlest men I have ever known.

Fred Copeman was one of the strangest characters I knew at Madrigueras. He didn't appear to have any particular function but raved around as a self-appointed officer. An exceedingly large and brutish-looking man he was popularly believed to have acquired a reputation as a heavy-weight boxer in the British Navy. Certainly, everyone was frightened of him as he charged around the place threatening to beat everybody's brains out, and looking as if he was quite capable of doing it. Unfortunately there was nobody around who was large enough to take him on with any prospect of success and he got away with it. He made himself out to have been the leader of the Invergordon mutiny in 1931, but in fact he must have played a very minor role as he was never charged with any offence after the mutiny was subdued. He later achieved his ambition of commanding the Battalion where he was universally detested. On his return to England in 1938 he was converted to Moral Rearmament, and then to the Catholic Church, and in both he was for a short time a prize exhibit as a converted Communist. He later wrote a book which is a farrago of nonsense and self-aggrandizement.

Another particular crony of mine had been the cartoonist of the *Daily Worker* who had always shown one of his favourite victims as George Vth. This caused a lot of resentment at that time, when it was felt that the monarch should be immune from ridicule. Poor Rony was freer of malice than most people but he was not to be deterred from treating any public figure whatsoever as a subject for satire. His cartoons were about the only breath of humour which drifted briefly through the *Daily Worker*, and his death on the first day in action left it the poorer. I don't know how much they paid him for his work but it must have been very little, because when I had known him in England he had always been completely broke.

One of the minor celebrities at Madrigueras, although he was never employed in any ranking job, was Christopher Sprigg. I have often seen it written that he used the name of Caudwell while in Spain; in fact he was always known as 'Spriggy' amongst his companions. He was an exceedingly modest, pleasant man whom I knew simply as a private of infantry like anybody else. I only learned subsequently that he had written five books on aviation technology, three books on philosophy and economics, together with *Illusion and Reality* which still remains one of the important books on Marxist aesthetics. In addition, he had produced seven detective stories and yet, when he was killed on the first day at Jarama, he was still under thirty.

Frank Ryan – one of our prestige figures – had apparently been a prominent member of the IRA since the days of the First World War, and a hero of the Easter Rising and all the subsequent battles fought for Irish independence. He had acquired a great reputation as a fighting man and, whilst still a Republican, had become an ardent Socialist. An apparently slow-thinking man, about fifty years of age, tall and heavily built with his head sunk into his shoulders, he seemed to have very little in common with the command of the Irish platoon: he remained with the British Battalion when the Irish left us, but appeared to have no particular function. He was taken prisoner with Harry Fry's No. 2 Company and remained in captivity when all the others were subsequently released. No one really seems to know what happened to him, but it is believed that he was held prisoner for several years. Hugh Thomas in *The Spanish Civil War* states that he died in hospital in Leipzig in 1941.

The machine-gun Company was put under the command of Harry Fry, a tall, very good-looking man of about twenty-eight who was, I believe, a shoemaker from Glasgow. He had enjoyed very little formal education but had a natural genius for organization and his company was by far the most efficient unit during the training days. His was the only company billet which was reasonably clean, his men worked hard and were full of enthusiasm. He was an exceedingly pleasant man to talk to and I used to spend a lot of my spare time in their billet in order to get away from the dirt and grumbling in the cinema.

It is difficult to assess the percentage of Communist Party members in the Battalion because those that were had been ordered to conceal their membership. In fact it was usually quite easy to pick them out by their specialized jargon and by their trick of prefacing any form of disagreement with the phrase 'Yes, Comrade but. . . .' My impression was that not more than 20 per cent were Party members and that the ones in the ranks were drawn from the lowest echelon of the Party structure. As far as I know, nobody was invited to join the Communist Party while in Spain. Everyone was bombarded with propaganda which was received with varying degrees of enthusiasm and I imagine that some people did apply for membership. This was particularly true of those with military ambitions as it soon became obvious that the hierarchy would only trust their own members in any senior position. But I personally knew of no one who was accepted as a Party member while we were in Spain.

Until my arrival in Spain I had known no Communists except on the basis of casual acquaintanceship. Heaven knows – there were plenty of them around, but those I came into contact with were either bores or unattractive people. Their literature seemed to me to be so hopelessly turgid and pretentious that I had never cultivated any of them. I had enjoyed a wild summer affair in 1936 with a young American communist, who was liable to start up on the subject of the workers –

frequently at the most inappropriate moments. I had discouraged this by making an appeal to her lower instincts which usually distracted her attention so that I had not really taken in very much of what she had to say on the subject of politics. Now, in Madrigueras, I became close friends with a number of fellows who were dedicated and obsessed Party members.

One of their most trying characteristics was their conviction that the Party must always and invariably be right on every line they took. My own idea was that Communism was concerned with the desire to build a world of social justice in which every man enjoyed a sufficiency of this world's goods and was given the opportunity for education which would enable him to develop his natural abilities to the mutual benefit of the entire community. I was swiftly disabused on this score and discovered that my concept of Communism was written off as mere bourgeois idealism. I had always imagined that idealism and idealist were words of approbation but here they had become anathema. I was genuinely and sincerely shocked. However it was explained to me that I had the whole thing back to front, Utopia arrived eventually as a product of history. It was only necessary to conform with a natural and inevitable process of history in order to assist rather than obstruct the inevitable. The works of Marx, Engels, Lenin and Stalin were as much Holy Writ to them as the Bible is to Christians. The revealed truth was there and any attempt to resist it was mere perversion. I now learned about the doctrine of 'revolutionary expediency', propounded by Lenin, which still forms the basis of Communist morality and ethics. In its simplest form it is that the end justifies the means, as long as the end is that of advancing and consolidating the Revolution. This doctrine lies at the root of Russian foreign policy but also governs the manoeuvrings within the Party and within the alliances which it forms from time to time. Its application produces a complete reversal of any kind of morality to which I had been accustomed. Nothing is good or bad absolutely, but only in terms of whether it is good or bad for the Revolution. For instance, it is not only good, but admirable, to make a friendship for the sole purpose of destroying the friend, if the destruction of that man will benefit the Party. The basis of the argument is that revolutions can only be made and maintained by a completely ruthless and single-minded attitude to every possible aspect of life. To a large extent I think that this may be true, but I doubted whether the social revolution produced by this method would be one under which I would care to live; in any case, I knew that I personally would never be able to convince myself of the justice of this point of view. I was not opposed to these Party-liners on ethical or philosophical grounds, but I was separated from them by a personal inability to accept their basic proposition. Apparently, I was a Marxist without being able to become a Leninist, and this, in the Communist mind, put me perilously close to being a Trotskyist which is quite literally a capital offence in any Communist organization. It would be possible to survive a charge of murder or almost any other crime in the calendar, but a man accused of Trotskyism would be certain of execution. This was a serious dilemma for I found that I was liable to be regarded as an enemy in my own camp.

5

In Training

So the days passed – to wake up in a damp and smelly billet with little hope of anything more than a very rough wash in cold water. Most of us had slept in our clothes to make up for the inadequacy of two thin, cotton blankets. Out into the cold wind and drizzling rain and the soupy mud of the main street to a breakfast of watery, milkless coffee with hard, dry bread and marmalade in the church, or if you had any money, cocoa and *churros* – the Spanish version of doughnuts – from the street-vendor on the corner by the Guardia Civil barracks. It was one of the great joys of life on the wet, cold mornings in Madrigueras to stop at his stall: he must have made a fortune out of it, but there was no official move to stop him. Everybody looking dirty and dejected underneath their groundsheet capes as we made our way up to the parade ground which had been the town square. Occasionally a Spanish peasant would go by with his long, black shawl wrapped around the lower part of his face, his broad-brimmed black hat pulled low over his eyes, minding his own business. There was an almost continuous drizzle of rain throughout the period of our sojourn in Madrigueras which made the whole of life a burden – the morning parade on the village square, the march out into the flat and dreary countryside, the tedium of the manoeuvres – all carried out in drizzling rain. In the billets there was no possibility of drying our clothing or finding a fire to warm ourselves. The evening meal, eaten in the church, never varied. It consisted of a watery stew made with whatever vegetables were available and a most inferior form of canned meat known to the French army as *singe*, where it was apparently the equivalent of English bully-beef. Its flavour was strongly reminiscent of carpenters' glue and, eaten cold, it was of a gelatinous consistency with traces of unidentifiable pieces of meat. Sometimes there was a pudding and always there was tea.

75

At this stage of the War it was always possible to buy food and drink but the problem of cigarettes soon became acute. The only tobacco available came in brown paper packages inside which were twenty little packets each containing sufficient tobacco to roll one cigarette. The tobacco itself was not very pleasant but the real difficulty was that it had merely been dried out and broken up small instead of being cut in the normal way, making it exceedingly difficult to roll into a cigarette. It could be managed in a dry place out of the wind, but on a wet day in the open it was virtually impossible.

Morning parade took place on the village square with proper military ceremonial after which the Battalion was stood at ease for the daily pep talk by Springhall, the Political Commissar. Every day without fail he opened his piece with 'Comrades, the position is as follows . . .', continued by a tirade of incredible nonsense, after which we were marched off on the vaguest and most ineffectual field-day manoeuvres that I have ever seen, particularly as we had no firearms of any sort. The manoeuvres were strangely reminiscent of my youth in the OTC, even to the use of rattles to simulate machine-gun fire, and I strongly suspect that they were derived from Macartney and Wintringham's experience of the same sort. We had no rifles which made the whole operation of giving covering fire to advancing groups a little absurd. But despite the rain and the mud and the general unreality of the whole thing, everybody did their best and remained fairly cheerful. It was unfortunate that we only learned to advance over open country – any other manoeuvre being considered negative in its approach to the problems of war. In the event, what we most needed to know was how to fortify a position and hold it, or how to beat an organized retreat, but neither of these things formed part of the curriculum, with disastrous results on the very first day that the Battalion was in action.

After the day's 'training' we were expected to relax with political lectures – or there was drink. The lectures were dreadfully dull and the only liquors available were grappa or anis to which the English were unaccustomed so that they became roaring drunk in a very short time. They disliked going without their beer. One platoon was told off every evening for police duties which principally consisted in rounding up the drunks who were thrown into the former Guardia Civil jail. They were paraded as defaulters on the following day and sentenced to various periods of imprisonment. This was felt to be very uncomradely and created a lot of ill feeling. No great harm was done, however, until a feud developed between the Irish unit and the platoon occupying the neighbouring billet. The feud developed until one night the platoon in question was given the police detail and arrested practically the whole of the Irish detachment, which led to mutiny. The Irish refused to turn out on parade and demanded that they should be transferred to the American Battalion. This seemed in principle a bad solution. The Irish should never have been put together as a national unit in the first place – it was an international force and although grouping in language units was obviously necessary on administrative grounds, grouping on national grounds was merely silly, and to put a purely Irish unit amongst an overwhelmingly superior number of English was inviting trouble. Most of the 'Irish' were not in any case from Ireland. The majority of them came from either Glasgow or Liverpool.

On this occasion – the first of several mutinous situations – a precedent was set for much that happened later. The mutineers were threatening to make all manner of revelations to the British press, and their bluff succeeded, to the great damage of discipline thereafter. It is an axiom in military affairs that it is easy to relax discipline, but very hard to tighten it after a long period of slackness. In the British Battalion, discipline was extraordinarily slack at the outset and subsequent attempts to tighten it always produced grumbling discontent. This sometimes approached active mutiny and the original purpose was never achieved.

During the training period J. B. S. Haldane arrived to instruct us in the art of handling Mills grenades. It was a poignant episode. The fact that we had none of these weapons, and never did acquire any more than the half-dozen defused bombs employed for instruction, was of no importance. Haldane was already a middle-aged and portly figure with his war experiences far behind him and it was my impression that he had never been a great expert on the Mills bomb. However, he was so pathetically anxious to be of service in any possible way that everyone treated the instruction as if it were a serious matter, and there was something rather touching in the idea of this very great and brilliant geneticist trying to make what contribution he could to our cause.

The grenades which were issued to us were ridiculous things. They consisted of a short length of mild-steel piping with half a stick of gelignite inside and a short piece of fuse sticking through the metal cap. The theory was that the grenadier lit the fuse and threw the bomb – it all sounded so magnificently simple. But it didn't work that way. The only thing we had to light the fuse with were the ordinary flint and tinder lighters which the peasants use to light their cigarettes – a flint and steel, as on a petrol lighter, with a length of yellow tinder cord impregnated with saltpetre. The system was to roll the wheel fiercely with the palm of the hand until the tinder caught a spark which was then blown up into a glow and applied to the piece of fuse sticking out from the end of the grenade, igniting it. After that you threw the bomb at the enemy. It was all perfectly simple – if you had time enough, if it was a fine day and the tinder had not got damp, if the piece of fuse had not become unravelled, and all the other ifs that made it an utterly impracticable weapon. The only advantage of it was as a morale builder, particularly with the bright yellow tinder cord braided up and worn over the shoulder like an aiglet.

After several weeks of being weaponless we started to receive a most extraordinary variety of automatic weapons. The first of these was always known as the 'shosser', and I never discovered what its proper title was. We were provided with a dozen of them for issue to alternate sections through the three infantry companies. It proved to be the most outstandingly useless weapon that I have ever seen and the entire lot were either lost or thrown away during the first day that we were in action. There seemed to be an almost unlimited number of ways it could jam itself, which it usually succeeded in doing before it had fired more than five consecutive rounds – the shossers had apparently been made in France for the French Army, and the French must have been wholeheartedly glad to have got rid of them. Every time the gun jammed it had to be entirely dis-assembled and put together again. They were not one of the Government's best buys.

For a brief time we were in possession of six, very elderly Lewis guns but just as their crews got used to handling them they were transferred to some other unit and were replaced with American Colts. This was a perfectly satisfactory weapon except that the ammunition belts supplied with them were so perished that they could not feed the guns efficiently. These too were all lost or discarded on the first day in action. It was said that they had been sold by the Americans to the White Russian army during the Revolution but the guns had gone to Archangel and the belts and ammunition to Odessa so that they had never met until now. Whether this story was apocryphal or not I don't know, but certainly the guns appeared to be unused and in their original wrappings.

The best of the automatic weapons which we received were eight Maxims. They were very old, none bearing a date later than 1916, but they were ruggedly constructed with a gun-carriage mounted on small, ironshod wooden wheels, a bullet-proof shield and a trail like a small field gun. They were too old to be really accurate but they were wonderfully reliable and completely formidable in defending the entrenched position where we were later to spend much of our time. The Maxims were handed over to the machine-gun Company to be used as the main support force for the three infantry companies.

When the Battalion finally went into action for the first time it was heavily armed with largely useless automatic weapons, apart from the Maxims. The remaining infantry was supplied with rifles of Russian manufacture. These were very poor weapons, much lighter than the English Lee-Enfield of that period and not nearly as toughly constructed. There was a short, chisel-pointed bayonet with a ring fitting and we were instructed that the rifle should only be fired with the bayonet in position. This was hopelessly impractical and all the bayonets were lost or discarded within a couple of days up at the Front. One of the radical disadvantages of this armament was that all the different types of weapon required different kinds of ammunition.

At the end of two weeks I became bored with the whole nonsensical business of training and manoeuvres and began to look for some more constructive activity with which to employ my time. The only useful thing that I had learned from the OTC was the construction of sketch maps, in addition to which I had the South African country boy's ability to estimate the range of a given object with a fairly high degree of accuracy. The total lack of maps was to be one of the severest problems that we had to deal with throughout the war. Francis – one of the Londoners I had first met up with at Perpignan – had picked up some knowledge of maps and mapping in the Boy Scouts and a new arrival, Michael Livesey, an architect from the Isle of Wight, was a valuable addition. I put the idea up to Tom Wintringham that we should form a small group to act as scouts. He was in favour, so I co-opted four of my Hackney friends from Perpignan and we became officially recognized. We paraded as a separate unit at the rear of the Battalion, and were attached to the Battalion staff during the daily manoeuvres. We were even permitted to set up a separate billet. We found space in a largish farmhouse, occupied by the head of the local village council and his daughter, Angelita. This was an enormous improvement over the dirt and stink of the cinema billet and life became more tolerable altogether. Whenever possible we brought back our rations from the cookhouse and purchased whatever small items were available in the village, handing them over to Angelita. In this way we were able to eat off plates with knives and forks instead of with a spoon out of a tin pannikin. We were able to launder our clothes and Angelita helped us to keep them clean and properly repaired.

Under these circumstances our morale improved enormously. Finding new ways to make ourselves useful, we were now enjoying ourselves. Some of the more orthodox Party members frowned on what they regarded as our 'bourgeois individualism' but we had created a useful role for ourselves and were tolerated on that basis. The first snag arose when we got lumbered with the 'Intolerable' Bee. Comrade Bee was a Communist in good standing and a natural bureaucrat. Before his arrival in Spain he had been employed as a draughtsman in the Sanitary Engineers Department in the Borough of Wandsworth. He immediately spotted our outfit as an ideal set-up for himself. Through his Party connections he managed to get himself put in charge of us and set himself up as head of the 'Cartographical Office'. He never appeared in the field but he was a real professional at erecting a mass of bureaucratic procedures which established him as an office man. He was expert at the arts of publishing memoranda, establishing procedures, issuing instructions and all manner of similar activities designed to bolster his own importance and to keep himself permanently indoors. Later on, when the Battalion went into action at Jarama, he succeeded in converting our original group of scouts into the Brigade Cartographical Office and set up an even larger and more pretentious establishment, miles behind the line at Morata, from which he never moved in the whole time that I knew him. It was one of the most extraordinary examples of bureaucratic skills that I have ever witnessed. However, Francis, Michael and the rest of us managed to get on with our own work and play without too much trouble from him while we were in Madrigueras.

We were paid 10 pesetas per day regularly every ten days, and this system continued even while we were at the Front. It is impossible to assess the true value of this amount as there was seldom anything to spend it on except drink and an occasional small luxury item of food. Later on, when I was in the American Battalion, I found that there was a great deal of obsessive gambling; this resulted in a few individuals amassing tremendous sums of pesetas which they were unable to spend, unless they could get to Madrid. There was nothing unrationed in the city except wine, women and song, of which there were plenty, easily obtainable with their otherwise useless pesetas.

The weeks dragged by, occasionally enlivened by a new draft from England with news and gossip to freshen the rather stale atmosphere in which we lived. In fact, I only spent about six weeks in Madrigueras but in retrospect it seems like months. During the last week we were joined by the British Company that had been fighting with the French Fourteenth Brigade on the Cordova Front, under the command of George Nathan. As it happened, the Company amounted to only about thirty men but we all turned out, wild with excitement, to welcome these almost mythical figures who had real fighting experience behind them. Some had been with the original Thaelman Brigade that had fought in the siege of Madrid and the University City in the early days of the War. But they had all been at Lopera, where Ralph Fox and John Cornford had lost their lives, together with many others whose deaths were less publicized. The propaganda machine had given a great build-up to the First British Company but it sooned turned sour, as it was now that we first heard the story which was to become increasingly familiar in the months ahead.

The battle at Boadilla had been hopelessly bungled. The troops had been assured that they would receive air and armoured support that never materialized. Communications within the Brigade had become altogether chaotic with impossible orders being issued, resulting in large and unnecessary casualties. During the post-mortem, somebody had to take the blame. André Marty, the chief Political Commissar, had

accused Lasalle – Commander of the Marseillaise Battalion – of being
a Franco spy and he was executed. Lasalle was a Communist of long
standing; he may have been a coward, he was certainly dandified and
pretentious with an exaggerated idea of his military capacities, but it
was manifestly absurd to maintain that he was in the pay of Franco.
The real purpose of the trial had been to assuage the fury of the rank
and file, who felt that they had been let down by the leadership. But it
hadn't worked. The men still felt that they had been let down and
nobody was convinced by the trial and execution of Lasalle. In fact, it
had only served to increase suspicion of the very people it was in-
tended to justify. We could not know that this pattern of unkept
promises of support, chaotic orders and communications, followed by
inquests, the finding of scapegoats and their execution as enemy agents,
was to underlie the whole course of events in the future. It was all
rather daunting to our unfledged idealism but at that time we were
convinced that it was all some kind of terrible mistake that could never
happen again.

One member of the First British Company has been seriously
maligned in the history compiled by those who only knew it at second
hand. Bert Ovenden had fought with Esmond Romilly and a dozen
other of the British attached to the Thaelman Brigade in Madrid and
the University City, and later at Lopera and Boadilla. During the whole
of this period he had been a private and was reasonably well thought of
by his comrades. He elected to stay in Spain and join the new British
Battalion but unfortunately he was now promoted. There is no doubt
that this was a mistaken appointment and that he turned out to be
hopelessly inadequate to the task, particularly at the battle of Jarama.
Nevertheless, he stayed with the Battalion and was killed at Brunete.
It is true that he failed in a position of responsibility, but he was a loyal
soldier of the Republic who fought as bravely as most others and finally
died in action. Nobody could have asked more.

It was announced that the Battalion was to be issued with rifles and
ammunition that very night and that we would be moving up to the
Front in the morning. It was still cold and damp as the men began to
pack their gear by the dim light of candles in their smelly billets, but
the general morale had picked up immensely. Somewhere around
midnight a convoy of trucks came rolling into the village and pulled up

outside a warehouse, into which the cases of arms and ammunition were unloaded. The word of their arrival passed quickly round the village and the men came drifting up with little flickering lamps and torches to stand whispering in the rain. The atmosphere was rather like that of the crowd that collects at a pit-head after news of a mine disaster – a compound of hope, fear and awe.

Finally the doors were opened and we filed silently into the dimly-lit warehouse. One by one we signed our names in an old exercise book and were issued with a rifle and bayonet and several packages of ammunition. One by one we filed out in silence, each man holding his new-found manhood to his chest. This was the real thing. All the degrading pretence of the 'training' was over and the reality of what we had come to do was upon us.

The Battalion paraded on the following morning with everyone self-consciously carrying a rifle which the majority did not even know how to hold in anything like a military fashion. For once, the idiot preaching of the Commanding officer and the Political Commissar was accepted with reasonable good humour. The rest of the day was spent in a sort of happy-go-lucky squad drill and although we still did not look like soldiers by the evening, we could at least move around without tripping one another up or bashing the next man's eye out with the muzzle of the rifle.

Late that night a convoy of trucks arrived to take the whole Battalion and its gear up to the railway on its way to the Front. Loading up in the dark with no very clear organization involved a lot of cursing and swearing and the giving of contradictory orders, but finally it was achieved. It was still drizzling when we left Madrigueras and I never saw the place again. Nobody could pretend that it had been a great success and I think that everybody was pleased to get out of it. I have no idea what happened to the unfortunate population of the village or their little bale of saffron. They had tried to be amiable to us because they were simple and amiable people, and I can only hope that they did not pay too high a price for it when Franco was victorious. They had never known anything but misery and I doubt if they ever will.

Just before we were due to leave for the Front we received news of the fall of Malaga and the hundred-mile strip of coast which the Government had held since the days of Franco's first advance. It was a narrow sector which was nowhere more than twenty miles deep: it had been severely bombarded and it obviously could not be defended indefinitely since the only access road at Motril was blocked by floods which had left the whole area virtually in a state of siege. The army of Queipo de Llano had opened an attack from the west on 17th January and advanced as far as Marbella, while a second army had broken through at Alhama. On 3rd February the attack reopened with the Italian Blackshirt armoured division advancing from positions due north of the city. The militiamen had no defence against tanks and armoured cars. The bombing was continuous and on 7th February the city and the whole coastal strip fell, and the usual story of the ghastly reprisals followed. It was a depressing prelude to our first action.

Many people writing on the International Brigades have described them as well-armed, highly disciplined and well-trained units. This we of the British Battalion certainly were not. My own experience, and everything that I heard at the time, leads me to believe that other battalions were no better. The trouble with any fighting body relying on propaganda for its organization is its chronic instability. In the case of a national army the emotions and sentiments involved are well founded in the life and habits of the individuals concerned, whereas this army had acquired its concepts in an atmosphere of enthusiasm rather than of experience or of calm consideration. It was assumed that, because we were volunteers and nobody doubted our sincerity in the cause, everything would turn out beautifully. Another fatal assumption was that sound knowledge of Marxist doctrine would enable the commander of a unit to make a wise military decision and that this knowledge would instil the necessary qualities of leadership. In reality the conflict between purely military and purely political decisions frequently arose and the resolution of them was seldom satisfactory. This particularly demonstrated itself in the selection of the leadership which nearly always passed to colourful bluffers, such as Macartney and Copeman. The theory was that they could be kept in line by their Political Commissars. Macartney had already demonstrated his incompetence before he was accidentally shot in the leg by Kerrigan, the Political Commissar, in an hotel in Albacete. Wintringham only lasted in command for a week before he was wounded, and thereafter Copeman was permitted to appoint himself to a position of command.

At no time was any attempt made to consider the welfare of the men. Owing to the absence of washing facilities for either person or clothing, the entire Battalion became infested with body-lice. No reading matter except propaganda was provided at any time, leading eventually to boredom and cynicism. And nothing was done to try and improve the deadly monotony and dirt of the food, which produced frequent attacks of diarrhoea. It is fantastic that no one in the hierarchy seemed to realize that dirt and boredom are the two most totally destructive forces in any body of men.

The British Battalion had started assembling in Madrigueras on 27th December, 1936. By 9th February, 1937, we had built up to over 600 men. Something over fifty of them had been in action on the Cordova Front, and the remainder had received some sort of training in Madrigueras but had still not fired a shot from any of their weapons. Only one Company Commander had been in action, and that, only as the second in command of a platoon. We possessed an assortment of automatic weapons of doubtful value as well as the Russian rifles. The Commander of the Battalion was well intentioned but totally inexperienced. The other three battalions which formed the Brigade were not very much better off. Whether Gal, the Brigadier, and his staff knew any more than the rest of us, I cannot tell. But it is quite certain that the Brigade was not the well-armed, well-trained force that various people have pretended it to have been. There was no lack of courage or firm intent amongst the rank and file but events were to prove that this was not enough.

6

The Road to War

The drizzle had stopped by the time we arrived at an unnamed marshalling yard which seemed to be miles away from any habitation. The train which had been provided for us consisted of a number of open trucks for the stores and machine-guns, together with half-a-dozen third-class passenger carriages for the personnel. The Battalion scouts were by this time beginning to experience some of the realities of soldiering. It was obvious that we were going to get very little sleep in the carriages so we volunteered ourselves as guards for the store trucks, and by arranging to sleep in watches every man got at least half a night's sleep in warmth and comfort, using his own blankets together with those of the man on watch. The night passed pleasantly enough as the train rattled along though a silent and apparently deserted countryside. We knew that within a few hours all the nonsense of training and manoeuvres were going to be translated into reality and every man had his own vision of what it would entail. My own notions were based largely on a *Boy's Own Paper* version of the 1914–18 War, coloured by a series of Hollywood war films. I knew that I wasn't going to like any part of it and wondered whether I would be able to summon up enough courage to acquit myself reasonably well. I found little confidence in my ability to do so.

The train banged and jerked around all night with frequent stops at deserted sidings. Francis and I had drawn the first watch until midnight, so that we woke up at sunrise when the train crashed to a halt at a small siding just outside Chinchón. The whole world had changed overnight. We were now away from the flat, dreary plain of Albacete into fine, hilly country: there was not a cloud in the sky, the sun was shining brilliantly and everybody looked keen and optimistic. Tiny Silverman and the cooks got to work to prepare some sort of breakfast while the rest of us unloaded our gear and sorted ourselves out into companies, ready to move off. We hung around for hours but eventually a convoy of trucks arrived onto which we piled ourselves and our belongings for the trip to Chinchón, which lies about forty miles from Madrid. Chinchón itself is a fascinating little town, famous for distilling the finest anis in Spain, and for the bull-run which is held every autumn in the beautiful, arcaded square which forms the commercial and gossip centre of the town. There was still no sign of war or any warlike activity and the few civilians around the place looked at us with complete indifference. Our stores were dumped in the middle of the square and a guard posted, while the remainder of the Battalion marched off into the countryside with the rifles and machine-guns which we were to fire for the first time.

More than eighty per cent of the men had never held a loaded weapon in their hands before. They had been shown roughly how to aim a rifle while in Madrigueras and now their total experience was to be the firing of ten rounds on an improvized range laid out on the hillside. Naturally enough it was not a very impressive performance. The 'shosser' light automatics quickly proved disastrous as they consistently failed to fire more than three rounds without jamming, and only the Maxim guns were really effective. Nobody seemed to be unduly depressed by the results achieved, but I could not see how we could possibly be expected to rout the enemy on our existing standard of musketry. No doubt we should be able to make a tremendously warlike noise but there seemed only a slight chance of our being able to kill any of the enemy, and wars are not won by loud noises.

At the end of the day we returned to Chinchón to rest up for our night march up to the front line. I think we all felt pretty uncertain of ourselves and of what the future might bring, but at least we had escaped from the squalor and futility of Madrigueras. We began to feel like men again and something of the spirit of the crusade came back into us. Had I realized that one half of our company would be dead within the next twenty-four hours, I might have felt differently. As it was, I felt afraid but uplifted. We had come to fight for a noble cause and we were now being given the opportunity to show our worth. I may not have grown up yet – but, as things turned out, it wouldn't take very long.

Tom Wintringham had now taken over command of the Battalion. Kerrigan and Springhall, the chief Political Commissars in Albacete, had disappeared and I never saw either of them again. Their place was taken by George Aitken, a quiet, modest and conscientious man who was consistently zealous for the welfare and just treatment of every man in the Battalion. I think that he suffered many struggles between his loyalty to the Communist Party and his sense of justice to the men. He behaved courageously and well in the initial disasters at Jarama and played a valuable part in keeping the whole show together after Wintringham was wounded. He finally returned to England and broke with the Party, but I have no idea what happened to him after that. Harry Fry was in command of the Maxim machine-gun Company, and Overton of the Colt machine-gunners. Jock Cunningham, who had fought with the original English Company, had No. 1 Company and William Briskey, a London bus driver and a very sincere and decent man, was in command of the other infantry company. We now had a leadership which was well liked and in whom everybody had confidence: a situation which had never existed in Madrigueras.

In the evening, the machine-guns and ammunition, together with the commissary stores and so forth were loaded into trucks to be transported to some buildings, about six miles away, which were to serve as the Battalion depot. They were to be accompanied by the cooks and commissariat. The scouts were to travel ahead with Wintringham and Aitken to discover a line of advance for the Battalion when it arrived on foot. The only trouble about the arrangement was that the Battalion had never marched so long a distance before – and they were now burdened with rifles and ammunition, in addition to blanket, packs and other impediments. A march of six miles may seem a pretty trivial matter, but these were mostly city-bred fellows who had been consistently undernourished during the years of the Depression and, in some cases, for generations. They would arrive worn out and would get very little sleep before going immediately into action. They were already tired as most of them had not slept on the overnight train ride. The prospects did not look very good to me.

The place selected as Battalion base consisted of a large house with farm outbuildings, situated on the road from Chinchón to San Martín de la Vega, which was in enemy hands. The road from Chinchón ran through the valley of the Tajuna river and the buildings themselves lay close under the slopes of the plateau which was later to form the Jarama Front. It was a fascinating house, still furnished in every detail but evidently unoccupied for several months; probably since the beginning of the War. The farmhouse itself was built around a large courtyard with shade trees and a well. There were a number of out-buildings, including the *bodega* where the winemaking had been carried on, and a huge labyrinth of cellars dug into the hillside. In this part of Spain they do not use barrels in winemaking, but huge pottery jars as much as twelve feet in height and about seven feet in diameter. The walls of the *bodega* were lined with about forty of them so that it looked like a set for 'Ali Baba and Forty Thieves'. The house itself was no ordinary farmhouse, as it had been the country retreat of Bogaria, the famous cartoonist of the old Liberal Party newspaper *El Sol*. Bogaria was a famous character in Madrid. A brilliant cartoonist and wit, a mighty trencherman and a boon companion, above all, he was admired as a man who had sufficient courage to continue a campaign of vicious opposition to anything of which he disapproved, through all the vicissitudes of life in the Spanish political arena. He was frequently arrested or beaten up but *El Sol* was an internationally respected news-paper that few politicians dared to close down. There were endless stories about the double-edged cartoons he had got past the censor to annoy or embarrass politicians of whom he did not approve. During the dictatorship of Primo de Rivera he was constantly in trouble and decided to protest against the frequent censoring of his cartoons. Each time one of them was censored he published a little 'design for needlework'. Everyone knew the joke and this peculiarly Spanish piece of humour made a nonsense of the censorship to the delight of the Madrilenos who are by nature the most irreverent people of Spain.

From the outside, the house looked like any other large, prosperous farmhouse with its entrance through a huge waggon gate into a farm-yard overlooked by a row of veranda'd rooms on the first floor. The front door opened from the courtyard into a large and well-furnished hall which appeared to have been the principal living room. Doors opened from it to a dining-room, a rather formal and dull-looking salon, and on to a stairway which led to the bedrooms above. It was all rather grand but the principal feature which relieved it were Bogaria's paintings which ran around the walls, through the barns, over the huge stone jars in the wine store, everywhere – including the lavatory. The drawings were without captions, nor did they need them. The majority were anti-clerical, all rather bawdy and exceedingly funny; sometimes a single composition on a wine jar and sometimes a series of pictures running around a room like a comic strip. The only part of the house which had not been used in this way was a bedroom which had been used by José Mejias Sanchez – the *torero* of Garcia Lorca's 'Lament'. The whole house had a thoroughly bachelor quality, and it appeared that this bedroom had been kept as a retreat for the *torero* to use whenever he wished and had subsequently been kept as a shrine of remembrance after his death in the ring. It was very simply furnished with a plain iron bedstead and a small dressing table. the walls covered with bull-fight posters, banderillas, swords and other souvenirs of his fighting career.

I had for a long time considered Garcia Lorca to be one of the very greatest poets of this century and had been deeply moved by the story of his brutal and senseless assassination only a few months before. The 'Lament for José Mejias Sanchez' is one of the loveliest of all Lorca's works, and here I was, standing in the room where he may have stood before he went out to meet his death – '*a las cinco de la tarde*'. I only had a few minutes to relish the experience before the rest of the soldiery arrived and in a moment the whole place had been stripped clean of souvenirs.

This lovely old house was to be the Battalion base, store and cookhouse and almost immediately it had become the filthiest and most bedraggled place in the country. All armies seem to be equally bestial in this, that they are not satisfied merely to pillage the houses through which they pass but seem to be possessed by some kind of hatred which compels them to actual defilement. English soldiers billeted in their own countryside during the last war showed the same urge to desecrate any place that they occupied. It is frequently remarked on as one of the standard horrors of war, but always with the suggestion that the army of one nation thereby seeks revenge against the civilians of another. I don't think this is true. Some kind of vandalism enters into a man's character the moment he puts on a uniform and is assimilated into the purely masculine world of the Army – any Army – which sets him against the civilian world whatever its nationality. This army, for all its idealism, was no exception.

The Battalion arrived at first light in more of a shambles than anything approaching marching order. The men were cold, tired and depressed. There was a hot meal ready for them but many were too tired to eat and simply lay down under the olive trees and went to sleep, without even removing their gear.

The general situation was that Franco's forces were making an encircling attack round the west and south of Madrid with the aim of cutting the highway to Valencia. The advance had commenced on 6th February on a front of eighteen kilometres, running north and south on a line parallel with the Madrid-Andalusia highway. For this purpose Franco had deployed the most highly-organized professional army yet seen in the War. Under the command of General Mola were eight mobile brigades, the majority of whom were seasoned Moroccan troops from the Army of Africa. In support of the infantry were six batteries of 155 mm. guns, the German Condor Legion artillery group of 88 mm. artillery, and a number of heavy machine-gun groups, followed up by cavalry and the Italian air force. Against this array General Miaja, who had remained faithful to the Republic, established his defence along the Jarama river as far as its junction with the Tajuna. Most of this line was held by ill-equipped Spanish units from Madrid with the XIVth International Brigade holding the left flank.

When we arrived on 12th February Mola's infantry had already crossed the Jarama river. The holding force around the bridges had proved inadequate and two of the bridges were still intact as the demolition charges had failed. For some extraordinary reason Mola had decided to launch his main attack up the sides of the Pingarrón hills along the line of the San Martín-Morata road. I recently visited this area and it is a complete mystery to me why Mola should have aimed his offensive at the exceedingly steep hillsides of Pingarrón, rising nearly a thousand feet from the flat valley of the Jarama river, when he could far more easily have swung his main line half a mile to the south which would have given him access to the valley of the Tajuna river. This valley is several miles wide and completely flat with a good road which would have enabled him to deploy his cavalry and to advance at great speed towards his objective, outflanking the whole Republican defence. In the event the offensive cost him 20,000 casualties and achieved no effective purpose.

Our Battalion now became part of the XVth International Brigade, designated a *Brigada Mixta*, that is, an infantry brigade with its own artillery and tank units and with medical, supply and transport organizations in support. It was a system introduced by the Russians, who had great faith in it. Basically it was conceived as an independent, mobile assault force, capable of rapid movement and entirely free of reliance on ancillary services. I do not know whether or not the military theory behind it was sound but it did not work out in practice. Owing to the shortage of replacement troops, once a unit was committed to a sector of the line it could not be withdrawn as there was no other to take its place. Later on, as the result of the military build-up, it became possible to use these special assault brigades in the way that they had been conceived, but the sad fact remains that they never won a battle. On every occasion that a new or reconstituted *Brigada Mixta* went into action as shock-troops, they suffered such tremendous casualties within a matter of days that they were no longer an effective unit. With us in the XVth Brigade was the Dimitrov Battalion of about 600 men, consisting of units drawn from practically every country in the Balkans, and the Franco-Belge Battalion, of about the same number. The Lincoln Battalion, of about 500 Americans, did not join us until 23rd February.

The Brigade artillery consisted of two old French 75s and one even more ancient English 5·2 Howitzer. Most of the gunners were French, and they established themselves in a position in the Tajuna valley just behind the Pingarrón range, from which they never moved in all the months I spent on this Front. I imagine that they were seriously short of ammunition as they frequently spent weeks without firing a shot. I never met one of their observers in the line and their shot usually passed far overhead to land somewhere in the valley behind the enemy lines. I very much doubt whether any of it was particularly valuable or effective. But they appeared to live a happy and peaceful life, busy with the cultivation of a fine vegetable garden around their gunsite.

We had a squadron of nine Russian tanks manned by 'Russian' personnel, though they were more likely to be refugee Communists from other countries who had been trained by the Red Army. These tanks were used as infantry support. If an infantry unit was hard pressed, a unit of three tanks was brought up to fire on the attackers. The tanks were always used with tremendous caution and as far as possible were kept in dead ground where they could not be fired on by the enemy, but could appear behind the infantry and loose off a barrage from their small quick-firing guns before falling back again. We possessed no anti-tank guns or mortars. The tank personnel lived a completely secluded life in a heavily wired and guarded compound well behind the line and never mixed with the rest of us in any way. The only one of them that I ever met was the Commanding Officer, a striking figure in a Russian cavalry uniform – a very smart affair with an overcoat that fitted tightly above the waist and with a huge flaring skirt finishing only six inches from the ground. Periodically, one of the despatch riders whose business took him down to their compound came back with all kinds of fancy canned goods and cigarettes with Russian labels, so it looked as if the tank men lived pretty well.

All staff officers of the International Brigades at this time were known as 'Russians' and some of them even wore Russian Army uniform. In fact, I do not think that there were any genuine Russians in Spain at all. Our 'Russians' were all Balkan refugees who had gone to the USSR and received their military training in that country. They habitually spoke Russian amongst themselves as a *lingua franca* and to distinguish themselves as an elite. The Chief of these was Brigadier Gal, by origin a Hungarian who had distinguished himself in the revolution in that country. It is improbable that Gal was his real name as most of the important Communists adopted pseudonyms while in Spain. I did not know him at all well, as he left the Brigade to become Divisional General after the first couple of weeks at Jarama. He was a man with a pleasant, easy manner, but I had the feeling that the other Russians plotted together against him. Certainly Copic, the Brigade Political Commissar, appeared to dislike him and he was held responsible, I think unfairly, for the failure to carry through a successful attack at Jarama. I know that George Nathan liked him and was happy to serve as his Chief of Staff.

George Nathan had made such a good reputation for himself in command of the English Company on the Toledo Front that he had now been appointed Chief of Staff of the newly-formed XVth Brigade. He is the only personality serving with the International Brigades who emerges as an authentic hero figure, with a mythology of his own. A number of individuals of all nations behaved magnificently but none of them had the essential larger-than-life quality that distinguished George Nathan. However, the legends which have grown up around him bear little relation to the man as he really was. The myth of his gold-topped swagger-stick which appears in practically every book on the Civil War is a typical example. What he really carried was a good, solid walking-stick – a very practical and useful object for climbing over rough mountain territory. Another myth continually recounted of him is that he rode around the hills of Jarama on a 'magnificent charger'. In fact he always travelled around at the Front on the pillion of a despatch rider's motor-cycle, simply because that was the most effective transport available. Naturally there were no roads up on the hills amongst the rough scrub and olive groves, but a good and determined rider could always find a route – albeit a rough one – anywhere over the hills, far more quickly than someone on horseback or in a car could. It is true that Nathan was something of a showman, but most certainly there was nothing of the clown in his make-up. He was always im-maculately clean and well turned out in the Spanish Regular Army uniform without embellishments of any kind, as befitted the totally dedicated, military professionalism which was the basis of his life.

Physically, he was well above normal height, broad-shouldered and slim, with a very erect and military carriage. His features were un-mistakably Semitic: long-faced, with a rather hawkish nose and black, curly hair. He had the most tremendous stamina and appeared to be completely impervious to physical exhaustion. I never saw him carry a weapon of any sort and although the wearing of large pistols had become a status symbol among those in positions of power, he regarded it more as an encumbrance than an asset. He had an excellent and ready sense of humour, together with enormous charm. Probably his greatest merit was his magnificent air of authority and decision. His self-assurance was so complete that he never felt the need to shout or to give orders in anything other than a quiet and normal voice. And I have never heard of his orders being questioned, as he possessed the gift of being able to instil into others the unquestionable certainty that he knew what he was doing and that it was for the best.

It has often been said that he was a homosexual. While it is true that he did build up a personal entourage of chauffeur, batman and so forth which may have been suspect, he always behaved with such admirable personal discretion that there was certainly never any overt suggestion of homosexual tendencies. Thirty years ago people felt much more strongly about these things than they do today, and had there been any serious hint of something of this sort at the time, he would have never emerged with such an untarnished image from the history of the period.

He was neither a Communist nor a mercenary. It was not in his nature to think deeply on political questions but was content to trust his own feelings, and I knew him well enough to know that he believed strongly in the justice of the cause for which he thought he was fighting. He was a Jew of working-class origins but was almost totally unconcerned with Judaism or class sympathy. I am quite certain that when he resigned his hard-won commission in the British Brigade of Guards, after the First World War, he can only have done so as a matter of principle – his exceedingly strong sense of sympathy for the under-dog. Nathan's special quality was his pride, which he nursed as other men nurse their most precious possessions, and it was the greatest form of pride that I have ever known for it would not permit him to perform any action which was below the immaculate standard of perfection which he had set himself.

All this may seem a little bit too good to be true but the man was well known by several thousand officers and men over a period of two years. Most of them were very tough characters indeed. Many of them were fanatical Communists whose very instinct caused them to mistrust a man whose characteristics of speech and behaviour derived from essentially upper-class attitudes. Nathan made no attempt to conceal his lack of political enthusiasms in any Party sense. The whole army was riddled with intrigues between factions out to destroy one another, but in spite of all these things Nathan emerges from the history of these events as the only person who was universally admired.

When the Brigade was formed, Vladimir Copic (pronounced Chopich) was appointed as its Political Commissar. He was a Croat, reputed to have been a Communist Party member of the Yugoslav Parliament before he fled to the USSR and entered the ranks of the Red Army, and was the most consistently disliked and mistrusted of all the 'Russians' in Spain. He was an utterly unprincipled brute who would swear that black was white if it suited his convenience, and his only genius lay in his capacity for intrigue. He later managed to put himself in command of the Brigade and held that position to the end, in spite of a series of more or less disastrous failures, by always shifting the blame on to somebody else. While I was on the Brigade staff, he always treated me civilly enough but he was an oily little bastard and I hated him. One of his least attractive characteristics was that he fancied himself as a grand opera singer, and I was part of his captive audience. It is said that he was executed in one of the Stalinist purges after he returned to the USSR.

The Brigade Intelligence Officer was Stephanovitch, a tall, handsome man who I came to know better than any of the others, as he spoke fluent English. He was always very amiable to me and I saw quite a lot of him as the map-making organization came under his immediate control. But he seldom appeared to have anything very much to say in public or at staff meetings. Yurani Yuraslav was supposed to be the Brigade Communications Officer, but his entire equipment consisted of a dozen old field telephones and a few rolls of very antique wire so that there was not very much that he could do in the event and he soon disappeared.

The Battalions each had a quarter-master who obtained part of his supplies from the Brigade stores, situated at Morete de Tajuna and part of it by local purchase, so the whole Battalion was largely dependent on his energy and initiative in shopping around for local vegetables, oil and wine to vary the diet. In this respect the French battalions were magnificently served as their quarter-masters appeared to be able to procure a variety of commodities which we never saw. Except for the special goods reserved for the 'Russians', the Brigade stores had almost nothing to distribute in the way of food or clothing—there was flour for bread which was baked in the village bakery, but very little else. Each battalion had its own Medical Officer and there was a field service clearance hospital behind the line with further hospital organizations at Colmenar de Orega and Tarancón.

Theoretically the common language of the Brigade was French, a language which none of the Brigade staff nor any of the battalion commanders spoke with any real fluency, except for those of the Franco-Belge Battalion. To make matters worse, the bad French spoken by a Russian or a German is quite unlike the bad French spoken by an Englishman or an Italian. People could just about make themselves understood in ordinary life but in the heat of battle, over an inadequate telephone line, there was virtually no communication at all. This problem was solved by one of the most remarkable collections of human beings in history. There were altogether about fifteen interpreters of various nationalities. None of them spoke less than five languages, some of them working happily in ten. Apart from their duties as interpreters they were employed as despatch riders, telephonists and anything else that was called for around the Brigade Headquarters, and without them the whole organization would have fallen to pieces. One of the reasons why Nathan always rode pillion on a despatch rider's motor-cycle was that he thereby ensured that he would always have an efficient interpreter by his side, wherever he went. Five of the interpreters were White Russians from Paris who must have been brought from Russia by their parents while they were still children. All of them were seized with a burning desire to return to their mother country. This had nothing to do with politics but was simply derived from strong national feeling. They each felt that by joining the International Brigades they would establish a sufficient reputation for good-will towards the USSR to be allowed to return to Russia after the War. Whether any of them succeeded in this purpose, or what finally happened to them, I never found out.

I came to know the whole group very well and loved them dearly, but my most particular friend was Hans. He claimed to be a Pole by origin and a safe-breaker by profession. His English was highly idiomatic and almost entirely accent free. He spoke ten other languages, apparently with equal perfection. He never seemed to be afraid of anything or anyone and had sufficient personality to talk back to André Marty, the demented Political Commissar who was responsible for a series of arbitrary executions. Hans was always cheerful and amusing and did a great deal for me when my morale was almost broken after those first days of the battle.

But even with such an outstanding group of interpreters there were still plenty of misunderstandings. In the heat of battle the Brigade staff members were largely dependent on word-of-mouth reports in order to follow the progress of activities at the Front. These often became incoherent in the excitement of events, and frequently had to be orally translated into three languages without time for careful consideration of their wording. Misunderstandings were inevitable and sometimes resulted in absurd and impossible orders being conveyed to commanders at the battalion level. Understandably, this led to a lack of confidence in the Brigade command and to mistrust of one another within it.

7

The First Day at Jarama

As soon as it was light enough to see what we were doing Wintringham assembled the scouts and we set off to explore the situation ahead of us. Our only instructions from Brigade Headquarters were that our sector would be to the south of the Morata-San Martín road and that the enemy were held up by the river forming our western Front. Francis and I climbed up through the steeply-rising olive groves in the early morning sunshine. The whole world looked clean and sparkling after the sordid misery of Madrigueras and its surroundings. Ahead of us, we could hear the sound of desultory firing but in this peaceful and almost idyllic setting it was hard to believe that it had anything to do with a war. The countryside appeared to be entirely deserted of people or animals. The peasants had all moved away and the opposing armies had not yet made contact with one another. The hills were planted with nothing but olive trees, about eight inches in diameter and lightly pruned, so that they gave a pleasant, dappled shade on the thin, whitish soil which had apparently not been cultivated that spring. There had been a light frost during the night but the climb to the top warmed us up.

Here we found a fairly even plateau about two kilometres in depth, falling away steeply to the Jarama river valley ahead of us. The sound of firing was becoming slightly louder and a few spent bullets whistled overhead. In spite of the brilliant, early spring sun, it was still cold, but the frost was rapidly thawing and the visibility was perfect. We made our way forward talking and smoking as if we were on holiday. Finally we came to the edge of the plateau where the ground fell away sharply and the olives finished. Ahead of us was a steep slope covered in rough growth about eighteen inches high. There was a secondary ridge about

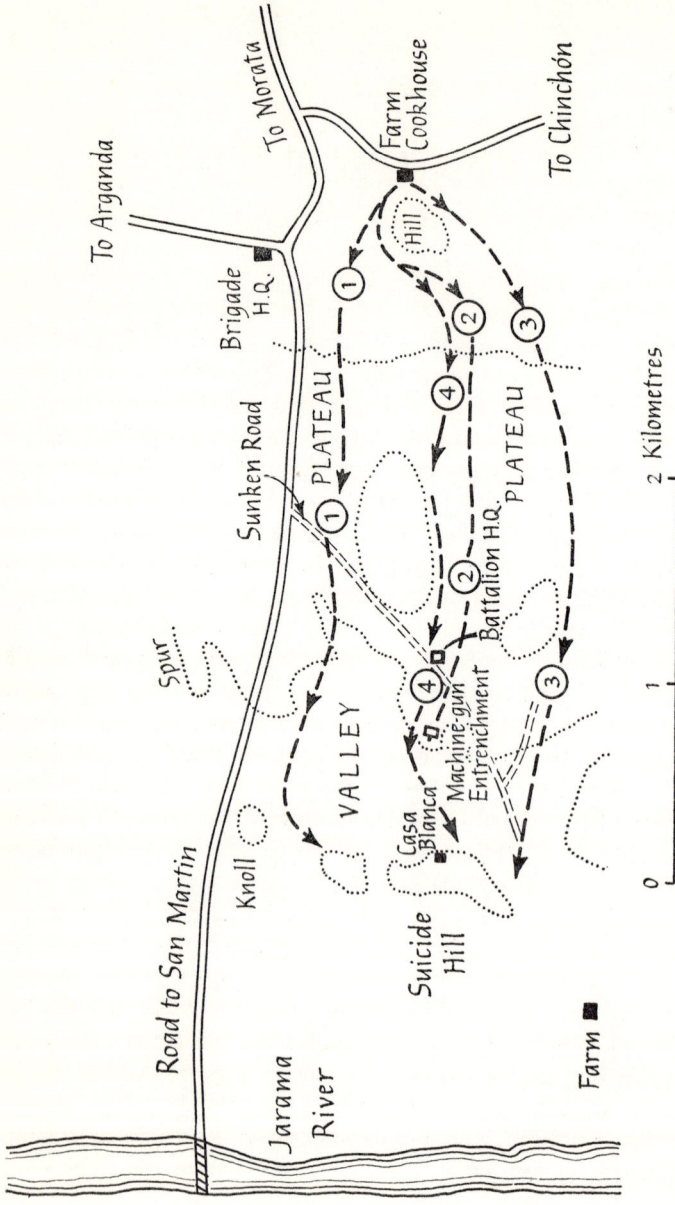

Sketch-map of the Battle of Jarama indicating the advance of 12th February

half-way down the slope with a small, white house on its highest point. We marked this on our maps as Casa Blanca. It later became known as 'Suicide Hill', but before the War was over there were 'Suicide Hills' all over Spain. About two miles ahead was the Jarama river with the village of San Martín de la Vega lying another half-mile back. It was obvious that Franco's forces had already crossed the river in considerable strength and that this hillside would be the site of our first battle. Yet we still felt no great sense of urgency, beyond the pleasant feeling of excitement one gets before a paper-chase or something of that sort. We just sat down with our notes and drawing boards, working away with an occasional glance at the enemy below. We had completed as accurate a sketch map as was possible under the circumstances when we ran into the Brigade Commander with his retinue standing atop the escarpment. In the valley below, about two miles away, we could see the river and a bridge. It was impossible to make out any detail at that distance as by now an early morning haze hung over the bottom of the valley. The Brigadier explained to Wintringham how his companies should advance, instructing him to move them as quickly as possible before the enemy could cross the river in strength. It was all rather like a school field-day.

Looking back it seems fantastic that not even the Brigade staff possessed maps of the area in which they proposed to fight a major action over steep country on a sector several kilometres in length. There was no single point from which they could observe more than a part of the action in progress, and they were dependent on reports arriving in four different languages. Under these circumstances I think that it must have been quite impossible for Gal to have had any very precise idea of the state of affairs at the Front from his position at Brigade Headquarters, where no part of the action was visible at all. Nathan, constantly travelling all along the Front on his despatch rider's pillion must have been the only person with any clear idea of the overall picture. Francis and I had prepared a reasonable sketch map of our sector and Wintringham was using this during one of Nathan's appearances among us. As a result the Battalion scouts were later transferred to the Brigade staff where we became permanently employed.

We were still standing alongside the conference of Brigade and Battalion staffs in suitably respectful attitudes when suddenly Francis let out a yelp and cried out, 'God, I've been hit.' He had been struck by a stray bullet from somewhere away down in the valley. We all turned to look at him as he stood holding his left arm with his right hand and the blood pouring out over the cuff of his coat. Everyone seemed to feel that it was rather bad form to interrupt a polite occasion in this way. I had never seen anyone shot before and the whole thing struck me as somehow being faintly improper – here we were, standing miles from anywhere, on a beautiful spring morning, when all of a sudden Francis gets his arm smashed up by someone he has never even seen. We had been brought up on the wrong books. The bayonet charge 'over the top' in Flanders seemed fair enough – you expected to get killed or wounded, and you did – but there was something vaguely unsporting about this. I patched him up with a temporary splint and a field dressing, and a despatch rider who was going down to the rear took poor Francis on his pillion. He was our first casualty, and I never saw him again or heard what happened to him.

While this was going on a large number of aircraft appeared at high altitude. They were opposed by a squadron of fighters and a terrific dog-fight ensued. This was the first time that I had seen aircraft in action and it was very thrilling. But again it was all rather unreal – a bit like watching a film. We were far enough away to be in no possible danger, the roar of engines and rattle of machine guns was terrifically exciting – but it was hard to imagine that men were killing and being killed up there in the sky.

At about 9 a.m. the Battalion appeared, marching by companies in column. There was a lot of laughing and playing around while the platoon commanders tried to keep order without getting tough; the whole thing looked more like a Sunday school outing than an army. Nos. 1 and 3 Companies were to deploy and advance to the Casa Blanca hill and the knoll; No. 4 Company to deploy and advance down the right-hand slope with the San Martín-Morata road as their right flank; the machine-gun Company to dig in along the head of the escarpment to give covering fire and to act as a reserve. As we went into action, No. 1 Company was commanded by Kit Conway, an ex-Naval rating, as Cunningham – their normal commander – was in hospital with influenza. Conway had been with Nathan in the first British Company that served with the French XIVth Brigade at Madrid and later on the

Cordova Front, in both of which engagements he had distinguished himself. Unfortunately, both he and Alfred Campeau, the Second in Command, were killed during the first day in action and no real leader appeared from the ranks to replace either of them until Cunningham returned from hospital a few days later. No. 2 (the machine-gun Company) was under the command of Harry Fry, whose sympathetic understanding and charm made him the most popular officer in the Battalion, and No. 3 Company under William Briskey, the London bus driver. He was a pleasant and kindly man who was killed in the first few hours of the battle. No. 4 Company was led by Overton who turned out to be totally ineffectual as a company commander.

We went into action plentifully supplied with machine-guns and light automatics but they were of four different kinds, and each required different ammunition; yet another type was needed for the rifles. The shossers and Colt guns were evenly distributed throughout Nos. 1, 3 and 4 Companies at the rate of two guns per platoon which should have been a formidable armament. However, Wintringham, in his book *English Captain*, makes it perfectly clear that he already knew that the Colts were useless and that the shossers were little better. In the event, all these weapons were discarded within an hour of the enemy advance and were all left behind when the companies retired from their initial positions. The Maxims were old, and somewhat inaccurate, but could be kept firing indefinitely as long as they had cooling water and ammunition.

A hundred yards to the rear of Harry Fry's position on the edge of the escarpment was a sunken road, whose surface was about four feet below the general ground level. It ran roughly parallel with the line of the enemy's advance and joined the main road from Morata to San Martín. Here Wintringham set up his Battalion HQ which consisted of himself, the scouts – of whom only four remained – and a telephone to Brigade. This was to prove more of a liability than an asset. Without any maps and the use of map references, it was practically impossible to describe the situation with any degree of accuracy. Moreover, the line and telephone equipment were in such poor condition that any conversation was so mutilated as to be almost incomprehensible.

These sunken roads are a prominent feature of the Spanish country-side and played an important part in every military action. They have been formed over the centuries by mule or ox-carts cutting up the earth along the tracks. Washed away by the winter rains and blown by the winds of summer, they become slightly deeper every year. In most places they are only three to four feet deep, but vary according to the local climate and soil conditions. From the military point of view, they provided ready-made entrenchments in which men could take cover and move around in comparative security. Their disadvantage was that the men, having found this haven, were understandably unwilling to leave it. And because they were as straight as circumstances permitted the original carters to make them, they were totally vulnerable to enfiladed fire.

Everyone took up their positions and the whole situation appeared to be perfectly sensible and well under control. Until about 10.30 a.m. there was a certain amount of light musketry fire but nothing to cause serious alarm. The whole slope down to the Jarama river was pretty steep and it was obvious that Franco's forces could not hold any position short of the plateau on which we stood, or they would be defenceless against fire from the higher ground. Eventually they had either to advance across the plateau or to retire back across the river. By now we could see a continuous skirmishing line on our side of the river where the enemy was fighting with their backs to it and had only one small bridge across which they could retreat. It was obvious that this was going to be a bloody and hard-fought affair, but the propaganda machine had so reduced the reality of the situation that we were convinced that we had only to advance for the enemy immediately to retreat. There would be one or two outstanding examples of gallant conduct, and everything would be fine. Nobody at Madrigueras had said anything about artillery fire or the genius of Moorish infantry to move across country without presenting a target for anyone but a highly-trained marksman – a category that included no one in our outfit. In the event, we were utterly unprepared for what was going to happen to us.

Fry had kept his men busily working all through the morning cutting a trench and setting up positions for his guns. They had no tools or sand-bags but somehow or other, using bayonets as picks and tin helmets as shovels, they had dug themselves into a reasonably safe fortification about a hundred yards long around the edge of the plateau. They had worked out the fields of fire and calculated the siting of their guns to a nicety. The only snag was that the truck carrying the guns and ammunition had not arrived. The other three companies spread out along the hillside, preparing to make an advance in the best tradition of our Madrigueras training. Everybody was full of confidence, as we now had real machine-guns instead of rattles, and every man had a rifle even if he did not know how to use it in any effective manner.

One of my duties as a member of the Battalion scouts was to act as Wintringham's runner. During the course of the day I made several trips down to the Brigade HQ, situated in a shallow stone quarry about a mile back, along the road to Morata. It was all very impressive. The Russians were standing in a group around Brigade Commander Gal. In one corner of the quarry there were half-a-dozen operators with a collection of antique telephones and wires coiling around in all directions. Messages were being received and orders despatched in a variety of different languages. Despatch riders were coming and going in all directions: a whirl of activity, centred on the person of the Brigadier. George Nathan was away up in the line, so one of the interpreters took me across to the Command group and presented me to Stephanovich, the Intelligence Officer. I presented my sketch map of our sector and explained the positions which we had taken up and the apparent position of the enemy forces. Stephanovich spoke a few words in English to show willing, after which he reverted to Russian through the interpreter. The Russians gathered around and broke into a furious altercation. I got asked a series of questions through the interpreter, but it was difficult to hear what he said above the stream of Russian argument that was flying around my head. Eventually there was a pause and Gal gave what was clearly a momentous order. Duly translated, the order was that the Battalion should advance immediately along the whole line of our frontage. I explained that we had still made no contact with the Franco-Belge Battalion, who were supposed to be occupying a position on our right flank, and was told that they were already in position and had commenced their advance. I knew damned well that this was nonsense as I had come down via their supposed position, but who was I to argue with a Russian Brigadier?

I grabbed a cup of coffee from one of the interpreters on the way out and set off, back over the hills. By pure accident I lighted on the Maxim guns and ammunition which belonged to Harry Fry's machine-gun

Company, lying in a fold in the ground behind the sunken road. They had been brought up by truck and unloaded in a place which was admittedly well concealed, but the truck driver had gone off without informing anybody of their whereabouts. Amongst the rest of the gear were two large *bidons* of wine which I took with me. These I delivered to Harry with the news of his guns and ammunition. The wine was as welcome as the guns, since the whole Company had been digging all morning without anything to drink at all. This lucky break improved our whole situation enormously. We now had a central redoubt armed with eight reliable Maxim guns and 120 riflemen in a fortified position with a clear field of fire over the whole Battalion sector.

I got back to Wintringham's HQ and relayed the Brigadier's orders. Runners were sent out to 1, 3 and 4 Companies to order the advance. I went up to No. 2 Company's trench to observe their movement and report back. William Briskey's No. 3 Company on the Casa Blanca hill was the first to move down the hill from its summit, followed shortly after by No. 1 Company under Kit Conway. But I could see no sign of Overton and No. 4 Company as they were concealed from me by a fold in the ground. Suddenly, and without any warning, all hell broke loose under a storm of artillery and heavy machine-gun fire. It concentrated first on the Casa Blanca hill, which became completely obscured in clouds of smoke and dust. Gradually it spread right along the line of our forward positions. The barrage was continued for about three hours. From my position in Harry Fry's trench I could see the chaos of Casa Blanca hill, where some of the men were working away with bayonet and tin helmet in an attempt to produce some sort of fox-hole in which to hide. None of the Colts or shossers were firing, and very few rifles, but the enemy were lying in concealed positions and had not yet started to advance. Our men seemed to be fascinated by the little white house which was already in ruins. They kept moving towards it, presumably because it was the only solid cover in the district, and seemed undeterred by the fact that the enemy were using it as a ranging mark, and that it was there that the shelling was heaviest. No. 1 Company seemed to be a little better off in their position on the knoll. They had a nucleus of experienced men, under Kit Conway, and found a certain amount of cover on the reverse slope. But from both positions there was a continual trickle of walking wounded and stretcher-bearers making their way back from the Front. Some distance away, we could hear a tremendous battle going on to the north of us, but there appeared to be no action on either of our immediate flanks and we got the impression that we had been left on our own to fight a private war. Our prospects didn't look very encouraging. We knew that ahead of us was a considerable force with a far greater fire power than we could muster, and the situation started to lose some of its field-day light-heartedness.

During a lull in the firing, Wintringham sent me down to the Casa Blanca hill to get a situation report from Briskey as we had received no word from him since the barrage started. I went along the sunken road and made my way across the dead ground in the rear of the hill. The firing had died down considerably but was still heavy enough to be frightening. When I reached the crest of the hill, the scene I found was really horrible. Briskey was dead and No. 3 Company had lost more than half of its total strength, either dead or wounded. The survivors seemed to be in fairly good heart but very angry. Some of them were trying to scratch some sort of cover for themselves and cursing the lack of any tools; others were trying to clear jams in the wretched shossers – spare magazines had become hopelessly clogged with dirt and had to be emptied, cleaned and reloaded. Everyone was asking for water. The situation in Overton's Company was worse. They had had equally heavy casualties but seemed to be making a much less serious attempt to prepare for the attack which must surely be imminent, and I could get no coherent sense out of Overton himself. He had a list of totally impossible requirements: reinforcements, artillery support, food, water and God knows what beside, but seemed to be making no real effort to keep the Company together. I had just got back to the sunken road when there was a storm of musketry. The enemy had started their advance.

I found Wintringham up in No. 2 Company's trench and told him what I could of the situation. As we sat there we were able to watch the Moorish advance. What was left of our three Companies were showing tremendous spirit but there was no machine-gun fire and only the occasional bark of a shosser letting off a few rounds before it jammed again. There must have been at least three battalions of Moors and their movement was amazingly skilful. Bobbing up and down, running and disappearing again, while all the time maintaining a continuous and accurate fire. They had to travel more than two thousand yards up an exceedingly steep hill with no apparent cover. They were the scruffiest looking soldiers I have ever seen; their uniform covered by a brownish poncho blanket with a hole in the middle which appeared to flutter around them as they ran. The rest of their outfit consisted of a rough brown head-cloth and a pair of rope-soled, cloth-uppered *alpagata* shoes which, if they weren't very military in appearance, were ideal for skipping around on that slippery hillside. It was terrifying to watch the uncanny ability of the Moorish infantry to exploit the slightest fold in the ground which could be used for cover, and to make themselves invisible. It is an art that only comes to a man after a lifetime spent with a rifle in his hand, whose very existence depends on his capacity to find safety where none apparently exists.

The effect of those brown, ferocious bundles suddenly appearing out of the ground at one's feet was utterly demoralizing. There appeared to be thousands of them popping up and disappearing all over the place, but seldom visible for long enough for anyone to get an effective shot at them. They were professionals, backed by a mass of artillery and heavy machine-gun fire supplied by the German Condor legion. It was a formidable opposition to be faced by a collection of city-bred young men with no experience of war, no idea of how to find cover on an open hillside, and no competence as marksmen. We were frightened by the sheer din of the battle and by the numbers of casualties. After the first few days I became indifferent to the noise, which was far louder and more furious than anything I had previously experienced. It was so intense as to seem to have an inescapably destructive force of its own. The horror of seeing close friends and comrades being killed and broken did not really penetrate my mind until later. It was all too fantastic for immediate realization, like something seen in a nightmare.

It was soon apparent that our situation was degenerating rapidly. A number of stragglers had come in with tales of the ghastly slaughter the enemy artillery had inflicted on our men out on the Casa Blanca hill. There were no reserves apart from the machine-gun Company which was perfectly sited to cover a retreat to the ridge. This began to appear inevitable. Indeed, had 1 and 3 Companies been ordered to retreat from their positions on the hills to the general line at the edge of the escarpment, all might have been well. But retreat was an ugly word, and they were ordered to hang on. These were completely raw troops, imperfectly trained and disciplined, ordered to hold a position on an exposed hillside against heavy artillery fire. They had no entrenching equipment, nor had they received any instruction in fortification. So they just had to hold on and endure it as best they could. In front of them were considerable forces of Moorish infantry, the finest infantry at Franco's disposal. It was obvious that as soon as the artillery had finished their softening-up process the infantry would attack. It was true that they were in a tactically inferior position as they would be advancing up hill over open country, and if our automatic weapons had been effective they would have suffered terrific casualties. Unfortunately the shossers had proved completely disastrous in action and the Colts, which were efficient weapons in themselves, were almost entirely useless owing to the supply of defective ammunition belts. This had been suspected before we went into action but since ammunition was short, we had not done enough practice firing to discover the extent of the defects until it was too late to remedy them. In the event, the men of the three Companies put up a very gallant defence but they were hopelessly outnumbered by enormously superior troops, and very few of them survived to retreat.

The situation remained more or less unchanged until late afternoon. It was a ghastly experience to sit in the comparative security of Harry Fry's trench and to watch the gradual but remorseless destruction of men with whom one had lived in conditions of peculiar intimacy in the billets in Madrigueras. Wintringham had tried to persuade Gal to agree to withdraw to the line of the sunken road – but the line must be held 'at all costs', any retreat would be met with court martial and all manner of dire penalties. One of the Russians arrived from Brigade HQ and put on a terrific turn in a mixture of Russian and incomprehensible French. By this time the question was becoming largely academic. There were very few of our men left on their original line and a huge body of Moors were advancing steadily up the hill.

Both Gal and Copic had a passion for orders of an arbitrary kind. 'You will counter-attack, regardless of circumstances,' capped by 'These are my orders,' and threats of court-martial and executions. Where they had acquired these habits I don't know. It is all part of the ridiculous attitude of mind that war should be a parade ground for courage;

whereas, it is usually something closer to a restraint of panic. Acts of courage do arise, but they are not part of the bread and butter business of fighting a battle, and the commander who expects to see them performed all the time and several times a day is a fool. At this particular moment we were a broken battalion. We had been beaten by heavier fire power, superior numbers and superior skills. The best that Wintringham could have hoped for was to prevent the men in his command from running away altogether. But to talk of making an attack with the battered remnant left at his disposal was merely absurd; to have court-martialled him for failing to comply with the orders would have been criminal.

Throughout the day a series of orders had been given, by telephone when it worked or by despatch riders, that there must be no retirement from the line which we had occupied in the early morning, and that reinforcements were being sent forward to strengthen our position for a counter-attack. In reality, except for the machine-gun Company, we were not effectively occupying any positions whatsoever. Seventy per cent of those who had been holding the forward positions were either killed or wounded. The rest were now without leaders, concealed in whatever place they could find to hide and wait for the opportunity of nightfall to slip away. As the sun set, the enemy at last appeared to have exhausted themselves, and they too were lying up wherever they could find cover. Gradually a few members of the three Companies came drifting back. All their automatic weapons had been lost or abandoned, and many of them had no weapons at all. Some of them stopped in the sunken road where Wintringham was trying to establish some sort of a line on either flank of the machine-gun Company. They were all in a state of greater or lesser shock, hungry and suffering from a tremendous thirst. Some of them stayed in the sunken road because they were too tired to go any further; others drifted right back to the cookhouse in search of food and water. The lack of officers among them made the situation impossible to control and no coherent military units any longer existed; just a collection of totally exhausted men.

On our left flank everything appeared to be quiet, although nobody knew exactly what was happening. Throughout the day we had never been able to make contact with the Franco-Belge Battalion which was north of the Morata road, more than a thousand yards to the right of our position. Why the enemy never realized this situation, or took advantage of it, is a mystery. Our left flank was completely open and as far as I was able to discover, there were no troops in that area at all, nor any reserve which could have been sent there. Fortunately the Franco leadership seemed to be obsessed by the road, and with the principle of destroying opposition in a face-to-face encounter rather than moving around the flanks, which would have been childs play to the Moors.

Since two o'clock in the afternoon it had been evident that the Casa Blanca hill and the knoll had been occupied by the enemy. A certain amount of machine-gun fire was coming from our right flank. The range was too great for their fire to be really dangerous, but fire from an unexpected direction always produces a certain amount of panic about being 'cut-off' – the perennial fear of all infantry men. However, once we had located the point from which it was coming everyone calmed down a bit, although it was obvious that Casa Blanca now formed part of the enemy front line.

Any battle boils down to the simple formula of the two sides throwing whatever they have got at one another until a point is reached at which one side gives it up as a bad job and retires. The Moorish infantry, with Condor Legion support, were throwing a lot more than we could deal with, and throwing it more effectively. They were hard, seasoned troops who were sufficiently experienced to realize that while our firing might be creating a considerable noise, it was not scoring a great number of hits. According to our theories, because the men on our side were inspired with a high ideal, we should be stronger than soldiers who were pure mercenaries. In reality, a mercenary soldier shows remarkable tenacity under fire because he is entirely committed to the military way of life and accepts its ethos – his pride is wholly concerned with putting up a good show as a soldier. He has real skill as well as courage, while we had only courage and good intentions.

The original leadership under Wilfred Macartney, Peter Kerrigan and Dave Springhall had evaporated before the Battalion went into action, and now most of the leadership at company and platoon level had been killed. The Battalion HQ remained intact but it was obvious that the command was hopelessly confused by events and did not know what orders to give. This situation was further disturbed by a self-appointed commander who charged around all over the place, giving orders to everyone on every subject. Fred Copeman, that great bull of a man, clearly visualized himself as a divinely-appointed leader by virtue of his immense strength – he had been a heavy-weight boxer in the Navy – although he was almost illiterate. Throughout his life he had used his fists to put himself in charge of any group of men he found himself among. He was completely without physical fear and seemed almost entirely indifferent to physical injury. On this occasion he was nominally in command of a machine-gun section over on the right flank, but had left them to their own devices, having received at least two wounds, one in the hand and the other in the head, which had been roughly tied up with field dressings. By this time he was more or less insane, giving completely inconsequential orders to everybody in sight, and offering to bash their faces in if they did not comply. Fortunately, he passed out at this stage and was carted away to the rear. Some days later he returned to the front and appointed himself unofficial joint Battalion Commander with Cunningham. When the latter was wounded later on, Copeman became the official Commander.

At one stage of the day's activities I was sent back with a message to Brigade HQ and instead of following the road, I took a short cut across the open country over which the Battalion had advanced during the morning. It was sad retracing our steps. The signs of indiscipline and of a totally unrealistic optimism lay on every side. The men were not physically fit and the stiff climb, combined with the morning sunshine, has caused them to abandon more and more of their gear, so that the whole olive grove was now covered with a mass of litter like an abandoned fairground. Most of them had evidently decided that the campaign would be over in a few hours and had left their overcoats, blankets, and packs containing spare clothes and personal possessions neatly stowed as if to be collected later in the day. Others had abandoned their belongings, item by item as they climbed the hill. There was an extraordinary variety of objects among the debris – hand grenades, ammunition, machine-gun spare parts, and clothing and equipment of all kinds. But the personal items which had been jettisoned provided the strangest part of the collection. Books of all kinds – though the Marxist textbooks, which were large and heavy, lay fairly near the bottom of the hill. The rest were of an amazing variety, ranging from third-rate pornography to the sort of books which normally fill the shelves of the more serious type of undergraduate. There were copies of the works of Nietzsche, and Spinoza, Spanish language textbooks, Rhys David's *Early Buddhism* and every kind of taste in poetry. But the rubbish mainly consisted of dirty paper, broken food and defecation.

On one of my trips I found a small cavalry carbine leaning against a tree with a leather bandolier of ammunition laying alongside. It looked as if its owner had put it down while attending to some other matter, with the intention of picking it up again later. He was now either dead or gone away. It was a beautiful little weapon for short-range work with a sling through the side of the butt to a fitting on the barrel, so that when it was slung over the left shoulder it lay snug to the body and left the right arm with full freedom of movement. It was short enough to enable a man to sit down without disturbing it. I was already disgusted with my Russian rifle. It was long and flimsy and impeded me as I scrambled around in the hills. The leather equipment with which I had been issued was uncomfortable and clumsy. The two big cartridge boxes on either side were always getting in the light and made work almost impossible, as I frequently needed to lie on my stomach. The bandolier belonging to the carbine was of well-worn and work-softened leather which was far more comfortable, and I was very much happier after the trade. My second acquisition was a short canvas coat lined with shorn lambskin. It was water-proof and wonderfully warm, although a little stiff and heavy, and was one of my most valued possessions as long as I remained at the Front. Unfortunately, it was stolen after I was wounded.

There was still no firing or any other sound of activity out on the left flank, and no one appeared to know or care what the position was in that quarter. If the enemy advanced around the blind side of the Casa Blanca hill they would be able to enfilade both Harry Fry's machine-gun positions and the sunken road, which would make our whole position untenable. Wintringham told me to make my way down the sunken road to investigate the position there. I had only gone about seven hundred yards when I came on one of the most ghastly scenes I have ever seen. In a hollow by the side of the road I found a group of wounded men who had been carried back from No. 3 Company's attack on the Casa Blanca hill. They had arrived at a non-existent field dressing station from which they should have been taken back to the hospital, and now they had been forgotten. There were about fifty stretchers all of which were occupied, but many of the men had already died and most of the others would die before morning. They were chiefly artillery casualties with appalling wounds from which they could have had little hope of recovery. They were all men whom I had known well, and some of them intimately – one little Jewish kid of about eighteen whose peculiar blend of Cockney and Jewish humour had given him a capacity for clowning around and getting a laugh out of everyone, even during the most depressing period, now lay on his back with a wound that appeared to have entirely cut away the muscle structure of his stomach so that his bowels were exposed from his navel to his genitals. His intestines lay in loops of a ghastly pinkish brown, twitching slightly as the flies searched around over them. He was perfectly conscious, unable to speak, but judging from his eyes he was not in pain or even particularly distressed. One man of whom I was particularly fond was clearly dying from about nine bullet wounds through his chest. He asked me to hold his hand and we talked for a few minutes until his hand went limp in mine and I knew he was dead. I went from one to the other but was absolutely powerless to do anything other than to hold a hand or light a cigarette. Nobody cried out or screamed or made any other tragic gestures. I did what I could to comfort them and promised to try and get some ambulances. Of course I failed, which left me with a feeling of guilt which I never entirely shed. There were no ambulances to be got, but I could not free myself from the feeling that I should have done something. To this day I do not know what I could have done to help those poor wretches as they lay awaiting death in the twilight of that Spanish olive grove. They were all calling for water but I had none to give them. I was filled with such horror at their suffering and my inability to help them that I felt that I had suffered some permanent injury to my spirit from which I would never entirely recover.

It was now almost dark. The enemy appeared to have packed up for the night along our original Casa Blanca line which was about 700 to 1,000 yards away, and far enough to preclude any sudden, unheralded attack. Nobody had eaten since breakfast, there was no water left to drink and everyone was dog-tired – physically and emotionally exhausted. But, at last, it looked as if we could now hope for a few hours of relaxation. However, our troubles were not yet over.

All of a sudden there came a crackle of musketry firing over our heads, from the rear of our position. After the first moment of panic it became obvious that this was not enemy fire. It was much too ragged and most of it was flying too high to be the deadly, professional work of Moorish infantry. The situation was not dangerous but it was very unnerving to us, particularly as we were all in a very jumpy state. We shouted and yelled at them '*Cameradas, aqui Brigadas Internacionales*', and a lot of less complimentary remarks, in every accent and idiom of the English language. Eventually they got the message, we were able to make contact with them and firing ceased. It appeared that they were part of one of our own Spanish battalions sent forward to reinforce the line.

Spain is a country that has always had compulsory military service and, presumably, all the members of the Spanish units had lived under military discipline for at least two years, but every Spanish outfit that I had to do with appeared to be devoid of any military sense. These were men of the Lister Brigade which was built up from the old 5th Regiment that had fought with such fantastic courage in the early days in Madrid. Contrary to popular belief, a great number of the officers held strong Republican views, and about half of them, from General Miaja down the line, had kept their oath of allegiance to the Republican Government and now formed part of our Spanish regiments. In spite of all this they looked and acted less like soldiers than any other bunch of fighting men that I have ever seen. They lay around the olive grove in a haphazard way with their rifles discarded beside them on the ground. Nobody seemed to be in charge of anything or to care very much what happened. Eventually a Platoon Officer came wandering up but he didn't seem to have received any definite orders, nor was he anxious for any. He did not know where the rest of his Battalion was situated, nor what form the projected movement should have taken. He had simply been told to move forward across the plateau and attack the Fascists. He had not adopted any particular formation nor sent out any advance patrols. He was sorry that his men had been firing over our heads but we had been invisible in the sunken road. Wintringham suggested that he moved his men up on to our left flank and he agreed to do this – but later. For the moment he and his men would stay where they were and refrain from firing in our direction.

We crept back into the sunken road which had, by now, become established in my mind as a haven of safety in a mad and dangerous world. Practically everyone had lost or abandoned their blankets during the day and it was now bitterly cold. I thanked God for the canvas and sheepskin jacket that I had picked up earlier, but I was too tired, both physically and emotionally, to be able to think coherently about the events of the day. First there had been the rather childlike excitement of moving up into the hills, seeing the enemy in the distance, the smoke of the enemy artillery fire from across the valley, staff officers and despatch riders rushing around in all directions, the aerial dog-fight and all the pure theatre of war with none of its dangers. This soon ended when Francis had been hit and the business started to become a little more real. Then the absolute crescendo of violence, fear and excitement as our three infantry companies had been pounded to pieces on the Casa Blanca and its attendant hill. But I had finally grown up into the reality of war only when I stood amongst that ghastly collection of dead and irretrievably mutilated men left behind in the retreat. This was the reality – not fear or excitement or drama – just pure horror and the knowledge that I was utterly powerless to do anything about it.

Finally I slept the sleep of pure exhaustion.

8

The Second Day at Jarama

It was bitterly cold during the night, but the sheepskin and canvas coat saved me from the worst of it and cushioned me from a part of the hardness of the road. I remember a series of nightmare-ridden periods of unconsciousness, punctuated by brief moments of wakefulness as the cold and discomfort forced me to move around. In the half-light before dawn I was jerked into full consciousness by the roar of an engine and a vast, looming monster bearing down on me. There was a moment of panic as I visualized myself squelched under the tracks of a tank. It turned out to be George Aitken – the only Political Commissar who was effective without becoming sanctimonious. Somewhere or other he had scrounged a huge, red truck into which he had packed about thirty stragglers who had made their way back to the cookhouse. These were some of the survivors from No. 3 Company. Devastated and lost after the attack on the Casa Blanca hill the day before, they had wandered through the night to the only refuge that they could think of, where George had found them. He had let them sleep for a while, giving them a hot meal and then brought them up to join us. With them he had brought a drum of hot, sweet coffee and a box of hugely thick bully-beef sandwiches.

It was bitterly cold and we were all stiff in bone and muscle after a hard night lying in the road. There were still occasional stray shots flying overhead but our condition of near-panic had subsided. Sunrise, food and a hot drink, and the sense that we were once again a coherent unit, braced our morale. But Tom Wintringham, who was normally very communicative, seemed to be totally confused. Anxious to succeed in the role of 'English Captain' in which he had cast himself, the realities had failed to live up to his imagination and he could no longer recognize himself. Fortunately, Nathan arrived on the pillion of a despatch rider's motor-cycle.

Immaculate as ever, strolling along the road and chatting with everyone as if the horror of the previous day had never happened, he struck exactly the right note – no formal condolences on our losses or political pep-talks, just an implied sympathy and a confidence that the whole situation was entirely under control. The Battalion still existed as a fighting unit even if there were not many of us left. We still had our machine-gun Company intact, and the presence of the only efficient automatic weapons which we had ever possessed, together with the personality of Harry Fry as Company Commander, gave us all confidence. Eight Maxim guns well dug in to a strong defensive position with efficient gun-crews, ample ammunition, all under the control of an officer whom everyone respected, was a very comforting thought. We overlooked the fact that they were supported by only 120 rifle-men and two officers, apart from the Battalion Commander. Overton had pulled himself together during the night, and André Diamond, the assistant quarter-master, was in great form, but there was nobody else. In the event, Overton collapsed again shortly afterwards, and André was badly wounded.

Wintringham picked up under Nathan's influence and began to take effective command of what was left of the Battalion. He sent Overton with about fifty men forward to the edge of the plateau on our right flank, and André with another fifty to a section of the sunken road, further up to the left where the formation of the land gave them a clear field of fire. The Spanish outfit in our rear had drifted off during the night, there was no sign of any force on our left flank, and we still had no communication with the Franco-Belge Battalion which was away to our right somewhere.

Once again the morning sky was bright and clear. We had all had a drink of hot coffee and plenty of food and everyone was busy preparing for the day. Above all, there was no serious firing and as the sun rose clear and brilliant and the chill went out of the air, there was still no sign of activity from the enemy. We could hear very heavy fighting away on our right flank in the Pingarrón hills, we could see a terrific amount of enemy activity in the valley below, but there was no sign of movement in the positions we had occupied the day before, except an occasional puff of smoke from a sniper's shot, and our own sector of the line remained at peace. One half of us cherished the hope that the battle had drifted away to the north of us, but behind this lay the horrid certainty that our time was coming. We were in a completely isolated position. Theoretically, the Franco-Belge Battalion was on our right flank but we had still had no communication with them and could not see or hear any activity from the position which they were supposed to be holding. I went down with George Aitken and his red truck to pick up the survivors of the party of wounded which I had discovered on the previous evening. Now that the Spanish outfit had left their position to the rear of the road, there was no sign of anyone for at least a mile. Franco's army always seemed to head for the point of maximum resistance rather than to move around an unguarded flank, but I did not realize this fact at that time and it looked to me as if we were in a thoroughly unsound position.

I made my report to Wintringham and went down to the Brigade HQ to make sure that they knew how the position stood. The British Battalion was holding the left flank of the Brigade and there was no telephone line to the Division, so that it was impossible to find out what was supposed to be happening beyond us. Gal, the Russian Brigadier, didn't seem to be particularly interested. Nathan was away up at the Front with the Dimitrov and Thaelman battalions who were under heavy pressure. The only useful fact I was able to glean was that the Franco-Belge Battalion was much further to our right than we had imagined, on the other side of the Morata de Tajuña road, leaving a gap of more than 700 yards between them and us.

When I rejoined the Battalion I found poor Tom Wintringham in the midst of an altercation with one of the Russian staff-officers. He had produced orders that the British Battalion was to launch a large-scale counter-attack to relieve the pressure on the other battalions on our right who were receiving a terrific battering. Aircraft were going to bomb the Casa Blanca hill and the other positions held by the enemy ahead of us. Tanks would move up on either flank. We were to be supported by the entire Lister Brigade (one of the most famous of the Spanish Republican units). There was at least a brigade of Moorish infantry in front of us with all their machine-guns and artillery intact; nevertheless, we were supposed to charge down the hill and drive the Fascists back across the river. It was nonsense.

Wintringham sent a few men forward through the olive trees but the moment they came into the open at the edge of the escarpment and met the mass of machine-gun fire ahead of them, they stopped: it was pointless to do anything else. In addition, the enemy now started to plaster us with artillery fire and it was obvious that it was them, not us, who were going to do the attacking. However, orders to advance continued to arrive, accompanied by threats and menaces from Brigade HQ. The promised aircraft and tanks had failed to materialize and there was no sign of the Lister Brigade. It seemed to me that with only a couple of hundred of us and eight machine-guns we would be damned lucky if we managed to hang on to our own 200 yards of front, let alone make a counter-attack that had no possible hope of success. Suddenly there was a terrific din from the machine-gun trench – shouting, cheering, a short fusillade of rifle fire and the dull thud of hand grenades. I started across towards the trench but our own Maxims opened fire in our direction and I ran back to the shelter of the sunken road. It was obvious that somehow or other the trench had been captured. I could not believe it. Now there was virtually no line at all except for the twenty or thirty men under the shelter of the road.

The official story of how the machine-gun Company's position was taken is still quoted in all its absurdity: the Moors came marching up the hill with their hands above their heads, singing the International and shouting '*Camerad*' until they reached the trench, when they produced grenades and captured the position. In fact, Overton's No. 4 Company on the right flank had retreated without notifying anyone. This enabled the Moors to creep up on to the high ground above and behind Fry's position, so that they could open an enfilade fire on the trench. This totally unexpected attack, apparently coming from their rear, took the machine-gunners completely by surprise and the entire position was overwhelmed in a few moments, whereupon the guns were turned on those of us remaining in the sunken road. Fry and about twenty of his men were taken prisoner but, except for Frank Ryan, all of them were released and returned to England a few months later.

The noise was indescribable. We were only about one hundred yards from the captured trench and the eight heavy machine-guns which it had contained were now turned on us. In addition, there must have been a couple of hundred riflemen firing high-expansion bullets. This was the first time that I had come in contact with this horrible and devastating weapon, the bullets of which exploded on impact with as much noise as a rifle being fired. Some months later I was myself wounded by one of these bullets and still bear testimony to the appalling wounds which they inflict. In size, the bullet is the same as that used in an ordinary rifle; it has no explosive charge but is, in fact, a super dum-dum. It is formed of a nickel alloy shell, in the point of which is a small slug of metal with a high coefficient of expansion, the remainder of the shell being filled with lead. The heat set up by the friction of impact causes the inner slug to expand more rapidly than the nickel jacket with the result that the whole thing explodes.

I think that at this particular moment we were all a little mad. The sheer weight of noise was tremendous and, coupled with a feeling of desperation and excitement, produced a kind of madness among us. People were running around shouting and behaving in all manner of peculiar ways. Wintringham bawled at us to fix bayonets, which was quite absurd. The original orders had been that in the line bayonets were to be kept permanently fixed since the Russian rifles were only accurate in this position. In reality the bayonets were such a bloody nuisance that almost everyone had discarded them. However, we all clustered against the bank ready to go over the top. It was rather like some totally improbable incident out of the *Boy's Own Paper*, and quite futile: a handful of men proposing to charge about two hundred yards into the face of eight Maxim guns and an unknown number of Moorish infantry.

Wintringham stood up to lead the charge, was almost immediately shot through the thigh, and collapsed into the sunken road. Aitken and about ten others jumped to their feet, scrambled over the bank of the road and charged. Very, very reluctantly I followed them.

I was running with my head down, presumably subconsciously imagining that my helmet would protect my face, and with absolutely no idea what I would do when, and if, I got to the other side. By the time that I had run about sixty yards I realized that there was no longer anyone in front or alongside me, and I dived for cover under one of the small hills built up around the foot of every olive tree. The heap of earth was only about eighteen inches wide and one foot high, but the eight-inch trunk of the tree provided cover for my head. This was the only part of my body that I was worried about at that particular moment and it felt as vulnerable as an egg shell. I had absolutely no confidence in my French tin helmet.

I was now lying in the middle of no-man's-land with rifle fire coming from both directions. I was familiar with the phrase 'to hug the ground', and I was now hugging it with a vengeance, as if I could press my way into it by pure force of will. My olive tree, and its minute hillock, gave me some protection from the front, but my backside was completely exposed to the fire coming from our own men behind me and I began to feel terrifyingly vulnerable. There was such an enormous mass of metal tearing at the air above my head that I dare not get up and try to run for the shelter of the road. I lay very close to despair. I had no thought of prayer, although I think that it might have been a very valuable consolation at such a time; nor did I think back over my past life, nor any of the other things that people are supposed to do in the face of imminent death. But I did feel very unhappy in no very specific way.

I wasn't frightened of being killed but of being mangled. The sight of a dead man did not cause me any particular distress; it was simply the end of a man which seemed to me normal and reasonable. But a living man, smashed out of shape, caused in me a reaction of the purest horror. To some extent this may have been because I was a sculptor, and the logic of the human body was for me one of its most exciting characteristics: the bone structure which maintains the basic shape; the articulation which enables the bones to operate around one another, but only in a limited and disciplined manner, making chaos impossible; the extensor and flexor muscles which act one against the other to control the movements. The perfection of the whole fascinated me, but the sight of the smashed and deformed living bodies at the end of the sunken road on the previous evening had shaken me badly. The thought of being torn and broken terrified me.

Finally my mind cleared sufficiently to arrive at conscious decision – if I stayed where I was, I was bound to be hit sooner or later, if I ran I might be able to reach the shelter of the road. I ran. I ran like hell and dived over the banking of the road and rolled to a stop on the far side of it. I have no idea how long I lay out in no-man's-land – time is not a factor in that sort of situation.

All that was now left of the Battalion was a handful of men rushing up and down the sunken road in a state of utter confusion. This was only increased when two Russian tanks appeared from the main road and started to bombard the Moors in the machine-gun trench. Their fire was erratic and there was a moment of panic when we thought that they were shooting at us. To be midway between a tank cannon and its target is a most unnerving experience when you hear it for the first time. The din of the gun firing, the roar of the projectile through the air and the explosion of the projectile on impact, all take place as one continuous sound – bang-buzz-bang. At first it is almost impossible to distinguish the noise of the gun from that of the projectile so you cannot tell from what direction the fire is coming. Only about a dozen rounds were fired, which added to the chaos but did not serve any useful purpose. It certainly failed to slow up the rate of fire pouring over our heads. The noise of a high-expansion bullet on impact is almost exactly the same as that of a rifle being fired. The bullets were bursting in the olive trees above our heads or in the ground or against whatever they struck, and the sound was completely bewildering. It seemed as if rifles were being fired from the trees over my head and out of the ground around me. There was no flash or other visible sign to tell me what was happening, and I really thought that I must be going mad.

It was the last time that I saw Rony, the cartoonist, and Hilliard, the boxing parson. They were both killed that evening. All that was left of the Battalion was about thirty men without automatic weapons, and no officers except George Aitken. One unfortunate individual who had obviously gone completely mad was rushing around enmeshed in a cocoon of insulated wire and crying, 'I have captured the Fascist communications, I have captured the Fascist communications.' Eventually he leapt up on to the parapet and was shot dead by a burst of machine-gun fire. My only feeling was one of infinite pity mixed with relief. It was horrifying, but it seemed to be the best thing, despite the fact that he had been one of my closest friends in the Battalion.

With the coming of darkness the firing gradually died down. The enemy were obviously satisfied with their day's work and had no intention of pressing on until the following day. I was by now physically and emotionally exhausted so I lay down against the bank of the road and fell into a deep sleep. Finally I was woken up by the intense cold of the night. Apart from a few dead bodies I appeared to be absolutely alone in the sunken road. This had been the worst day of my life. There was no point in staying where I was and I simply wandered off to look for the Brigade HQ.

9

On the Brigade Staff

It was still only half-light in the early morning when I found the Brigade HQ in a number of pits by the side of the Morata road. Nathan offered me some bread and coffee, which were very welcome since I had had very little to eat on the previous day. He told me to hang around as a runner. It was a beautiful day and for the moment there appeared to be very little firing anywhere in the sector, apart from the occasional crack of a rifle further up the road and the whine of a spent bullet overhead. The bloodshed and chaos of the previous day had not worried me at the time but now a reaction began to set in. My mind kept going back over the events of the last few days since the wounding of Francis; the waste and desecration of the olive groves, the finding of that ghastly collection of wounded derelicts and my inability to do anything for them, finally the killing and the total collapse of any semblance of order in the sunken road. I had often read about the sense of moral collapse which pervades a defeated army, but it was quite a different thing to experience it.

I must have been in a state of considerable shock at the time because I have no very clear recollection of the next few days. The polyglot despatch rider-telephonist gang took me under their collective wing and I soon began to recover. As far as I can recollect, I spent most of my time in their dug-out alongside the road but of the many changes which took place during this period I can remember practically nothing. Gal was transferred from the Brigade to take command of a division, and Copic, the Political Commissar, became Brigadier. Nathan had been transferred back to the French XIVth Brigade with whom he had served on the Cordova Front. His place as Chief of Staff had been taken over by a German called Klaus – an almost complete caricature of a Prussian officer. He was a man of a most offensive character, a natural bully who appeared to be in a permanent rage: shouting and yelling at everybody in sight and generally managing to be as unpleasant as possible. Personally, I never fell foul of him, largely because I took pains to stay out of his light. Klaus was later shot as a Nazi spy – which he certainly never was. If they had shot him on the grounds of being a first-class bastard it would have been reasonable, but as it was, he was executed as the scapegoat for one of Copic's mistakes at Brunete.

It began to look as if the Fascist drive on the Jarama Front had spent itself and that we were now settling down to hold a consolidated line on a permanent basis. The Brigade HQ moved out of the quarry on the roadside to a fine mansion about a mile further back along the road. In the meanwhile a small army of civilians was employed to dig a trench-line about half a mile back from our present positions, into which the Brigade could retire. Our men were far too exhausted and thin on the ground to dig any kind of effective fortifications in the position which they now held. In addition, the new line would be much easier to supply as it was on the edge of the reverse slope of the plateau, with dead ground behind it, whereas the existing line had nearly half a mile of flat ground behind it so that supplies could only be moved under cover of darkness.

I must have recovered considerably by the 22nd February because I distinctly remember my first encounter with the Lincoln Battalion. They came marching along the road, only about three hundred yards from the Fascist lines, concealed by a shoulder of the hillside and a bend in the road, and presented a startling appearance as many of them were wearing the 'dough-boy' uniforms of the 1914–18 War. There were about five or six hundred men dressed in what seemed to me an utterly bizarre costume belonging to the days of the silent films. And here they came, striding along with the apparent intention of proceeding straight on into the Fascist lines, just around the corner of the road. The explanation, as it turned out, was comparatively simple. The organization in the USA knew that there was a shortage of uniforms in Spain, so they had followed the simple expedient of outfitting the men from US Army surplus stores. Apparently they had been brought by truck to the junction of the Chinchón road with instructions to proceed along the road to their right, but nobody had told them how far to go. They had imagined that they would hear the thunder of a battle, long before they arrived. But it so happened that there was nothing more than a desultory sniping fire at that particular moment. What would have happened to them if they had gone on around the bend of the road, I dread to think.

They were led by a tall, bespectacled character who looked like a schoolmaster, draped in pistols, binoculars and all the panoply of war. He was very indignant when I came screaming down off the hill, shouting at them to stop. He seemed to think that this was a totally unwarranted interference with the script he had prepared for himself. Finally he agreed that perhaps I was right and proceeded to march the Battalion back down the hill again. I never got to know Tom Merriman well as he was wounded on his first day at Jarama. Most of the Battalion thought little of him and usually referred to him as the 'college boy'. He was certainly very determined to become a successful soldier. He came back as Commander of the reconstructed Lincoln Battalion at Brunete and was Chief of Staff when killed at Belchite. He must have been strongly supported by the Communist Party who put him in a position of command despite his lack of experience, and continued to back him although he never seems to have shown any outstanding military genius and was never very popular with the rank and file.

The Lincoln Battalion went into action on the following day. They took over the section of the Front which had been held by the Franco-Belges, and were thrown into a full-scale counter-attack in which they lost more than half of their total number without making any advance whatsoever. Merriman was wounded and his place taken over by one of those mystery men who seemed to appear at intervals in the history of the International Brigades. He was a red-faced Englishman with an exaggerated military manner who was always talking about the good old days in the 'Cherry pickers, old man' – apparently a reference to a fashionable British cavalry regiment. He answered to the name of Watters but who or what he was, I have no idea. He arrived in charge of a party of reinforcements and hung around for a few days at the Brigade Headquarters. Everybody treated him with great deference and one was given to understand that he was some kind of military genius. The Lincoln Battalion were very angry about the pointless slaughter on 23rd February but they received a number of reinforcements, all kinds of promises of air, artillery and tank support, and Watters as their commander. On the strength of this, they were persuaded to make a fresh counter-attack on 27th February. None of the support fire appeared, Watters ordered them to attack over and over again in the face of murderous machine-gun fire, and by evening only about 120 of them were left. Watters beat a fast retreat with half the Battalion swearing to have his hide. They pulled out of the line and refused to go back. Various members of the Brigade staff tried to talk them out of it and finally they agreed to go back into a different sector, but only under leaders whom they themselves elected. Martin Hourihan was elected Battalion Commander and Steve Nelson grudgingly permitted to remain as Political Commissar. Watters disappeared from view and I have no idea what happened to him.

The American counter-attack on 27th February was effectively the end of the battle of Jarama. It had lasted for only twenty-one days but had resulted in an estimated 45,000 casualties: 25,000 Republican and 20,000 of Franco's forces (Hugh Thomas's figures). Although General Mola's forces had successfully crossed the Jarama river and advanced some three miles, the attack had completely failed in its main purpose of cutting the road from Madrid to Valencia. From a purely military point of view it had achieved no useful purpose whatsoever.

It was true that we had succeeded in containing an offensive laid on by the finest troops that the enemy could muster, but the cost had been appalling. One of the slogans in the early days had been *Resistir y fortificar es vencer*: to resist and fortify is to conquer. At the time of the Jarama battle the authorities did not consider this a sufficiently aggressive attitude, but there is no doubt that had this policy been pursued for a little bit longer, until we could build up a well-armed and efficient force, the whole history of the war might have been different. Jarama was the ideal site for a defensive battle – a river backed by an exceedingly steep range of hills. Had we fortified along the edge of the escarpment before the bridges were lost, the enemy would have never been in a position to hold any of the valley land at all. Our casualties would have been comparatively low and the line could have been held indefinitely by a comparatively small force. The whole concept of containing the enemy's attack and replying with a counter-attack was ridiculous in itself, because everybody knew that we had no reserves with which to mount it, nor had we the armament strength to carry it out.

Since a condition of stalemate had now been reached, there arose the opportunity to try and rebuild what was left of the Brigade and to restore to it some measure of effective organization. The Brigade sector was now reduced to about five kilometres along the new trench line held by the remains of the four battalions. The Americans were on the left flank, and the British, Franco-Belge and Slav battalions occupied the right. With the Brigade HQ now housed in their small mansion about two kilometres to the rear, a serious attempt was made to put some order into things. The prime difficulty was the demoralization of the men – they had been so stuffed with propaganda that they could not believe that the disasters which had befallen them could have occurred without active treachery in the command. The doctrinaire clichés of the Political Commissars failed to satisfy them, and they were mutinous to a point where they threatened to march out of the line. All kinds of promises were made, cigarettes, food and mail made a miraculous appearance, unpopular faces were whisked away and everyone settled down to grumbling acquiescence.

We were now suffering the dreariness and misery of trench warfare in the rain. There was no longer any pretence of confidence in the command at any level, and all the little miseries that men laugh off in normal times became exaggerated into pure horror – the quality of the food, the lack of mail and cigarettes, and of any facilities to wash or obtain clean clothing, a thousand other trivial discomforts were all turned into matters for constant grumbling and complaint. The food was certainly much worse than it need have been. In practically every battalion the classic mistake of pushing the duds into the cookhouse had been made. The ingredients at this time were perfectly satisfactory but the stew which was all the cooks knew how to cook was brought up from cookhouses as much as a mile behind the lines, and was always stone cold and quite unappetizing by the time it was served out to the men in the line. Since there were no clean clothes or washing facilities it was not long before body-lice infested everyone in the trenches.

Personally, I was well off as far as the purely physical aspects of life were concerned. I was now permanently attached to the cartographical section of the Brigade staff. The food was good, I was warm and dry, there was no danger from snipers or mortar shells and there was even good company. The latter was amongst the interpreters and despatch riders. There were about a dozen of them who had their own mess and lived happily together. But Francis was gone, and Michael Livesey had succeeded in transferring himself to the XIVth Brigade with Nathan, so I was now without my immediate friends in the scouts. The bureaucrat, more pompous than ever, was in control. I loathed the brutish Prussianism of Klaus who could only communicate by shouts and grunts. The sinister figure of Copic, with his little, shifty eyes, began to get on my nerves. He was continually making remarks which could be read as being humorous or threatening. They weren't funny by any normal concept, and the feeling of menace in the man was very strong, besides which, his musical pretentions were intolerable. That I should be obliged to put up a show of a hearty appreciation for a lousy singer was not part of what I had come to Spain for. I started to look around for a chance to move myself into some other outfit where I could feel that I was justifying my existence.

I had welcomed the fact of being co-opted onto the Brigade after the disastrous first two days of the battle. It gave me the opportunity to rebuild my shattered morale and to recover from the state of pure fear which had reduced me to a point at which I was of no use to anyone. I was living in a place which was comparatively safe and comfortable. I was engaged in useful, if rather tedious work, drawing up a large-scale and detailed map of the entire Brigade sector. But it was now apparent that Franco had abandoned his attack in our area and we were settling down to a period of relative inactivity. I worked all day under the tutelage of the abominable Bee, who now enjoyed the title of Brigade Cartographer, and loved every minute of it. He had completely reverted to the world of petty and oppressive bureaucracy from which he had sprung, demanding respectful subservience to himself in the name of the Cause, on which he constantly delivered the most boring lectures. I suppose that he was a useful and sincere individual after his fashion, but he was the product of his environment, which was characteristic of everything I hated most.

One morning I got word that the XIVth Brigade under Nathan had come up in reserve and were bivouacked in the olive groves on the other side of Morata. It was typical of Copic's standard of military efficiency that there was no system of guards on the Brigade HQ area, so that there was no problem in coming and going as anyone felt inclined. I had no difficulty in finding one of the despatch riders to take me down there and I knew that I could always get a lift back when I needed it. I wanted to get myself co-opted onto Nathan's staff and away from the boredom and irritation of Copic. In the event, it was just as well that I failed, as Nathan and most of his staff were killed by a bomb not very much later.

The *Quatorzième* was an entirely French Brigade at this time but while it was on the Cordova Front it had been augmented by one English Company in which Nathan had distinguished himself, and the French held him in very high regard. They had all completed their national service and many had seen active service, either in the First World War or in Algeria, and they recognized the pure professionalism of Nathan. There is no doubt that the *Quatorzième*, as a fighting force, was as good as anything in Spain but its members seemed content to live in a state of utter squalor. When I found them they were scattered around all over the place, the ground was thick with discarded rubbish of all kinds, they were dirty and a fair percentage of them were drunk. The whole show looked utterly chaotic. I eventually discovered Nathan in a short length of trench with a tented roof where he had made himself and his entourage reasonably comfortable. He had with him still the two young Englishmen who he had co-opted as chauffeur and batman during the days in Madrigueras, as well as Michael Livesey, late of the British Battalion scouts, who could speak French and German, as interpreter. But the key to his organization was a most wonderful pair of knockabout clowns, Charpentier and Bubu, nominally employed as Battalion armourers. They were both very short, Charpentier, very thin, and Bubu, very fat. They were usually more or less drunk and constantly fighting between themselves, but their supreme virtue was that they were the most accomplished thieves in the whole of Spain. They would disappear for two or three days at a time and return with whatever was required, from a new motor car to a packet of razor blades.

The day on which I arrived turned out to be Nathan's birthday and they had felt obliged to justify their reputation. They had just appeared with a case of French champagne and other assorted liquor, several cans of Russian hors d'oeuvres, six partridges and four lobsters. All this was pretty good going, but the man who could succeed in stealing four lobsters in the centre of Spain during the Civil War was a real genius. They could cook as well as they seemed to be able to do everything else and we had a magnificent feast, the first decent meal that I had enjoyed since I left Paris, in spite of the fact that it was eaten out of tin pannikins, sitting in a hole in the ground. After dinner Charpentier and Bubu got down to some really serious drinking. At one stage in the evening Bubu suddenly leapt to his feet with a smart, clenched-fist salute and declaimed in a loud voice, '*Moi, toujours Breton et toujours Catholique*', whereupon Charpentier leapt to attention with an equally smart salute and yelled '*Et moimême, toujours Breton et toujours alcoolique*'. Bubu took offence, a tremendous row ensued, and they flew at one another like a pair of wildcats. There was a fairly considerable amount of superficial damage but five minutes later they were sitting down, covered in blood, with their arms around one another drinking and singing revolutionary songs together, Apparently this was a standard part of their drinking routine and nobody took any notice.

My plan to hitch my fortunes on to George Nathan was unsuccessful as he was only temporarily attached to the XIVth and, owing to his political position, was very uncertain of his own future movements. The Party hierarchy recognized his outstanding military qualities but, because he was not a Communist or willing to pretend to any great political enthusiasm, he was always suspect. On the following day the XIVth Brigade moved off and Nathan with them. He was killed by an aerial bomb at Brunete, and I never saw any of the gang again or heard what became of them.

Since my attempt to join Nathan and the *Quatorzième* had failed, I decided to try and hitch myself onto the Lincoln Battalion. In my role as Brigade observer I was up in the line every day and had got to know Marty Hourihan who had been elected Commanding Officer of the American Battalion after their mauling during their first few days in the line. The election was entirely against all Communist principles, but in that period of near-mutiny the survivors of the original Battalion had disowned the original CO and chosen Marty in his place. The situation had been so critical at the time that the political powers had accepted him and he had turned out so well that he became established as the official CO until he was wounded at Brunete. Martin Hourihan was a typical American. A tall, slim, loose-limbed young man of about twenty-seven with a face like a cheeky schoolboy. I don't think that he had had very much education but he was exceedingly intelligent. He was unflaggingly conscientious and although he could show considerable courage and toughness when necessary, he never threw his weight around, and I am convinced that there was not a single man in the battalion who did not like and admire him.

The American Battalion suited me much better than the British where Cunningham was nominally in command. Moreover, Copeman had returned from hospital and, although he had no official position, he set himself up as boss of everybody in sight. Neither of them had any sort of executive capacity. Their trench lines were the worst in the Brigade, from the point of view of both military efficiency and of sanitation. No systematic organization of dug-outs, communication trenches and latrines had been constructed, nor any washing facilities laid on; and the cookhouse had not been cleaned out or made efficient. As a result, the men were dirty and lice-infested, their clothes were permanently damp and they were ill fed. If I was going to move out of Brigade HQ, the Lincoln Battalion was clearly the best place to go. I therefore suggested to Marty that he should ask for me to be seconded to the Lincolns for liaison and interpreter duties. There was a good pretext for the latter role as he had no Spanish speakers amongst his own men and his left flank was held by a Spanish Battalion. We succeeded in working this transfer without too much difficulty, and I was released.

10

The Lincoln Battalion

I wanted to be alone to try and sort myself out before going up to join the Lincolns, and decided to walk rather than pick up a lift. I had no possessions apart from the clothes I stood up in, a blanket, a small haversack with a change of socks, singlet, razor, toothbrush and a couple of books. Since there was still no official uniform, I had been able to reduce my gear to a practical and convenient size. I had discarded the jacket of my original woollen ski-suit and replaced it with the sheepskin-lined canvas jacket which I had found on the first day at Jarama. When folded along its length it made a comfortable mattress for sleeping and a warm garment for night watches. The French tin-helmet had also been abandoned as I had seen so many with holes through them that I had no faith in any protection that it might offer. A khaki beret had become the general headgear, but I preferred the militia forage cap which was made of thin cotton and fitted more comfortably into a pocket. My original issue of boots were still in good condition and I had two pairs of sound, woollen socks. For the moment I was clean, but I knew that this would be hard to maintain up in the line and that I should inevitably become infested with the body-lice which were a part of life in the trenches.

By this time everyone up in the line was infested with lice: large translucent, yellow brutes which looked like sugar ants. They lived principally in the seams of any garment where they remained comparatively quiescent during the day, becoming violently active at night. Their bite produced large, raised weals that itched like hell. Up to now I had been able to avoid this particular form of misery. Down at Brigade HQ it was easy to keep clean and wash clothes regularly. But up in the line it was a very different situation. Most of the men up there had not moved out of the trenches for more than sixty days. Their bodies and their clothes were filthy. Water was scarce as it had to be carried up over the hills and Gal had ordered that no fit man was to be allowed out of the trenches, even for an hour, owing to the shortage of man-power. There was no insecticide and the only effective method of dealing with the lice was to run all the seams of your clothing through a candle flame at regular intervals. The lice popped and hissed in a most disgusting way as they and their eggs hit the flame, but the treatment was partially effective. It was a most depressing business to see civilized men squatting around hunting through their clothes and persons in pursuit of vermin like a bunch of apes.

It was a beautiful morning as I made my way up the hill. Most of the spent bullets and ricochets passed high overhead and there were only one or two places where they were dangerous. The larks were singing as happily as if it were peacetime and there were all sorts of small wild flowers beginning to appear in the crevices of what, in winter, had appeared to be utterly barren hillsides. I was already familiar with the terrain as I had visited it frequently in my capacity as Brigade observer.

The Lincoln Battalion HQ dug-out was in the dead ground on the reverse slope about seventy yards behind the main trench. Here it was possible to stand up and stretch without danger, but in the trenches themselves any careless movement was apt to be fatal. The dug-out had two bunks and Marty offered me the spare one as there was no regular Second in Command and no Adjutant. We only had about 120 men and such paperwork as needed to be done, was carried out by the quartermaster who lived down at the cookhouse, nearly a mile away.

It was now spring time. The rains had finished and there was bright sunshine all day, but it was still very cold at night. The particular area of no-man's-land opposite our lines was almost bare of olive trees but heavily planted with vines which now began to sprout in the spring sunshine. There were flowers everywhere and it all looked very pretty. The only snag in all this was that it would not be long before the foliage of the vines would obscure our view of movements on the enemy lines. My only duties were to make a tour through the lines every morning and evening and to report daily to Brigade HQ. There was seldom anything new and these duty tours were usually nothing more than a social visit. I started out on the left flank and had a drink with Ray, a cynic and a humorist who had made a great name for himself in the terrible days of the 24th and 27th February, but had no taste for discipline and liked to make his own rules. He later disappeared in most mysterious circumstances and it was rumoured that he had been captured and executed on one of his periodic desertions for a night out in Madrid. I then made my way along the trench stopping for a chat or a drink with various friends as I went. There was 'Frenchie' – there was nothing French about him and I never discovered how he acquired the name – who survived the War and returned to New York, Dave Polansky who was later killed as he stood by my shoulder in an observation sap, Oliver Law, a very fine and intelligent black Communist from Boston who later commanded the Washington Battalion and was killed at Brunete, the Flaherty brothers from Boston who succeeded in running the Irish Company – no mean achievement – and many others.

The Lincoln Battalion about 120 strong, contained a mixed assortment of characters, most coming from New England, particularly Boston, New York and Philadelphia. There was a high proportion of students – many of whom were writers and poets – and a few negroes, mostly well-educated and from the industrial north. There was also a Red Indian and a few Poles. Although the Battalion possessed eight Maxim guns, these were divided amongst the three infantry companies, and there was no separate machine-gun Company. The whole organization was fairly loose in character, and after the near-mutiny everybody had lined themselves up with whichever company set-up suited them best. A few of the original Irish outfit from Madrigueras had found their way to the Irish Company attached to the Battalion, but the majority were either Boston or Philadelphia Irish and had no real interest in Ireland as such. Some of them were not Irish in any way, but simply enjoyed the general atmosphere of the Company. It was commanded jointly and severally by Paul Burn and the two Flaherty brothers, all from Boston. This trio were quite inseparable and ran their company with a light-hearted but determined efficiency. One Company was predominantly formed of New Yorkers with a very high percentage of Jews and Communist Party members. They occupied the right flank of the position, and here the atmosphere was notably more puritanical and politically-orientated than in the other companies. The third Company occupied the left wing of the Battalion position and was formed of the real 'tough guys'. They were not over much concerned with politics, discipline or any other matter that came under the general heading of 'bull-shit', but clung to the idea of personal courage and endurance as the prime qualities of a member of the International Brigades. They were all men who had proved themselves during the really tough days at the end of February and would trust only men of their own kind. They gambled and drank more hard liquor than any other company, and had a higher record of temporary desertions to booze it up in Madrid, but they were the real hardcore of the Battalion when there was any fighting to be done. Here lived Ray and Frenchie and some of my best friends in the Battalion.

Steve Nelson, a big, tough shipyard worker from Philadelphia, became the Battalion Political Commissar, but Political Commissars were not very popular in the Battalion at that time and he never tried to throw his weight around. I think that he conscientiously tried to do his best for the Battalion at Brigade HQ but he never seemed to carry much influence. Certainly he never tried to interfere in the running of the Battalion and everybody was on reasonably good terms with him. He did not bunk with Marty and myself at the Battalion HQ dug-out, but preferred to live up with No. 1 Company, so we saw comparatively little of him. I got the impression that he was a very dedicated Communist, rather humourless and uncertain of the role that he was supposed to play in the affairs of the Battalion. He never seemed to be very active and was frequently absent for several days at a time. However, looking back on it I think he must have been responsible for the mysterious disappearances of a number of people from among our ranks and for the secret trials, for real or imagined offences, which caused so much fear and suspicion within the Battalion.

Doc Pike, the Battalion MO, was a youngish man who lived with his assistant in a dug-out behind the trench line. He obviously came from an upper-class New England background and appeared quite content to live an almost completely solitary life in his dug-out field dressing station. It was only large enough to accommodate two stretchers and a couple of wooden boxes, containing his stores and equipment. But, so far as the dust which filtered down from the road made it possible, it was as clean and efficient a medical unit as could be imagined. He never wore any badges of rank nor claimed any special consideration, which he could easily have done had he wished to do so. In spite of his rather solitary and unassuming way of life, he was a very friendly and amusing individual who appeared to have no deep political convictions, or at least he never discussed them. He seemed to be exceedingly able and conscientious at his job and I never discovered his reasons for throwing up a comfortable professional career in Boston in order to come out and endure the squalor of the trenches in Spain.

As it happened, I was exceedingly glad to fall into his hands when my time came. The British Battalion had no medical officer attached to it at the Front, and until a wounded man reached hospital the only medical attention he received was a field dressing applied by a stretcher-bearer, who had not even had the benefit of first-aid instruction. This could prove fatal, since he would be carried from the line down to the nearest road to wait for the first empty truck that came along that could take him to the nearest hospital several miles away. He might have a pretty good chance if he were one of the occasional casualties on a quiet front, but in the chaos of a major action his hopes were pretty slim if he was seriously injured and losing a lot of blood.

The Lincoln Battalion position formed the left flank of the Brigade and of the Division. To their left was a Spanish Battalion with whom they appeared to have no communication whatsoever. The line ran approximately north and south over level ground about a kilometre in length. Their right flank was held by the British Battalion but here again there seemed to be little communication between one another. This was one of the safest trench lines on the whole front as the trenches were deep enough to enable anyone to walk around below the level of fire. The machine-gun positions were well fortified and there was a truly magnificent system of dug-outs, in marked contrast to the miserable little burrows in which the British survived. The ground was a reddish conglomerate which was solid enough to support itself without timbering but soft enough to make digging fairly easy. The trenches nearly all had sufficient headroom for standing, with bunks dug into the side lined with mattresses made from mountain brush. They were all kept much cleaner than those of the British Battalion – indeed, some of their owners became so intolerably house proud that they would scream with rage at a cigarette butt thrown on the ground and insisted on the use of an ashtray. Sometimes it all became pretty silly but it relieved the monotony of trench life and afforded some degree of privacy in an otherwise over-crowded situation. There were communication trenches dug as far as the dead ground in the rear, and to the latrine pits which enabled the lines to remain reasonably odourless. We managed to get a fair amount of water for washing, but nothing ever beat the body-lice.

From a purely military stand-point, the trench lines were not ideal. They had been dug in an absolutely straight line across the hillside, so that if any one section had been overrun the remainder would have become untenable. No support line had been dug and if we had lost the trench which we held, there would have been no line to fall back on. Fortunately Franco lost interest in this sector, and the trench line held until the final surrender at the end of the War.

The Moors who had made the original attack had been withdrawn from the opposing line, and been replaced by regular Spanish conscript troops whose only concern seemed to be that they should be left in peace. Apart from occasional bursts of machine gun fire and the even rarer small mortar grenades, the only real nuisance was the snipers. On a stagnant front sniping is one of the few ways of alleviating the general inaction. The trenches were separated by a no-man's-land of only 200 to 300 yards, and the enemy were apparently well supplied with good rifles and explosive bullets. And so it was never possible to relax.

Neither side employed barbed wire or any other form of obstruction although attempts were made to rig up trip wires in no-man's-land, decorated with tin cans to give warning of a night attack. In reality, both sides were too weak to take any effective action against one another, and no serious attempts were made by either to advance the trench lines or to carry out any form of night raid. We were both content to accept the *status quo*. The only purpose of night patrols in no-man's-land was to relieve the boredom. On one occasion I went out with Ray and a couple of his men to cut down the young vine growth which obscured our view of the enemy trenches. We were creeping around in the pitch dark, breaking off the sap shoots, when we realised that our numbers appeared to have doubled. No word was said but both sides suddenly realized that they were working alongside each other on a mutual task. Nobody attempted to take any belligerent action, but each of us headed for home as fast as we could go.

Another way of surviving the boredom was by drinking. There was frequently a lack of food on Jarama, but never any shortage of liquor. There was a ration issue of red wine, and in addition supplies of prohibited brandy and anis were always available. Since it was impossible to stamp out completely, Marty turned a blind eye to the practice so long as it was kept within reasonable limits. This system worked very well – if somebody became drunk enough to be a menace, his mates pounded him into insensibility before there was cause for official action to be taken, and everyone else could go on with their ordinary social drinking without interference. We were lucky that we had no regular drunks, only kids who needed occasionally to break the tension of trench life.

On our side we had no mortars, but in the last few weeks before I was hit the enemy started using them fairly frequently. They fired a projectile rather like a small aerial torpedo and were not particularly dangerous although their nuisance value was quite considerable. We were all stretched to a high peak of nervous exhaustion and despite their size, the bombs produced a prodigiously loud explosion which was much more alarming than their lethal capacity warranted. For some reason they always seemed to fall in the area of the latrine trench, to the rear of the main firing trenches, and thus took their victims at a very serious disadvantage.

I soon settled down to my new life with the Lincoln Battalion and was comparatively happy. I made a great number of friends and was not obliged to live at close quarters with anyone I disliked. Marty and I got on well together and I was able to make periodic expeditions on various pretexts, to Brigade HQ. Sometimes I was able to get as far afield as the village of Morata de Tajuña, two miles behind the line, where life appeared to continue as if the War had never happened. The village itself was not very exciting, but it was very pleasant to be able to sit in a café drinking anis and chatting with the locals as if the War was a thousand miles away. It was all right for me, but for the majority of the Battalion, life was becoming very hard indeed, as month after month dragged by with no prospect of leave or any break in the dreariness, the dirt and the scarcity of food. Despite frequent rumours that the Brigade was going to be withdrawn for leave and re-organization, nothing ever came of it and people began to feel that we would be left to rot on in Jarama for ever. There was a lot of drunkenness and temporary desertions to Madrid for a couple of day's hell-raising provided a release for some. But everywhere there was a continuous and unrelenting grumble of discontent. One of our principle grievances was that there was no mail or news of the outside world which increased our feeling that we were forgotten men.

It was only now that people began to realize that nothing had been said in King Street about coming home, or even being given local leave, and no one had had time to think of it before. Now that the Battalion had been reduced to the level of a mere holding force on an inactive front we began to feel that the granting of leave was possible and that we deserved it. Approximately 800 men had passed through the Battalion between 15th February and 15th March, and now less than 200 men were left in the line. None of us had enjoyed a night's sleep out of uniform or a decent hot meal for several months. There was no relief from the continual fear produced by snipers and occasional mortar shells. We were filthy and full of body-lice and began to feel that we were in a trap from which there was no escape.

This situation produced a series of desertions. For many an unauthorized weekend in Madrid was not enough; they were determined to get out of the country altogether. Some of the deserters got as far as Barcelona, where they threw themselves on the mercy of the British Consulate, and at least one man that I know of made his way from Jarama all the way back to Figueras, over the Pyrenees into France, and eventually back to England. Some were captured, held in penal battalions and eventually released, but a large number disappeared without trace. How many there were nobody knows, nor what their fate may have been. Desertions became one of the principal topics of conversation – even talking about stealing a couple of days away from the trenches could reduce for a while the awful feeling of being trapped. Every Battalion in the Brigade was close to mutiny and if a man disappeared for a short time it was safer to pretend that nobody had noticed his absence for fear of making an official issue of it. Some people had disappeared altogether from the line, presumably for trial and punishment, and it was much wiser not to enquire what had happened to them.

I was now a student of the art of survival as I had no intention of dying for nothing. Snipers and mortars took a small but consistent toll, so that one became accustomed to the depressing experience of asking after a friend, only to be told that he'd been hit last night or that he had disappeared. It began to seem that we would sit up there in the dirt and stink of the Jarama trenches until we were gradually whittled away without having achieved anything at all.

It is a perfectly reasonable proposition to say to a mercenary army: 'Yours not to reason why, yours but to do and die.' Possibly it would work with any army of illiterate peasant serfs. But obviously it was no way to run an army composed for the most part of men who had joined up at great cost to themselves and who were prepared to make any kind of sacrifice for the cause in which they believed. They didn't mind what they had to put up with, but they expected it to make sense. In addition, they felt that they had the right to be treated as sensible and responsible individuals by the leadership.

In all the months that the Lincoln Battalion sat in the trenches on Jarama we had a Spanish battalion as neighbours on our left flank, but a buttress of the escarpment formed a division between us and neither side had sufficient interest ever to walk around it. For all practical purposes we might have been fighting entirely different wars. Not only was there no social communication, there was no official contact either. I went into their lines several times and tried to make friends, but they were always mistrustful and surly so I finally gave up. This saddened me very much. I sincerely believed in internationalism, almost as an act of faith, and here an opportunity for two peoples to know and understand one another was being entirely lost. The only member of the Spanish Battalion that I got to know was an orphan boy, about ten years old. He had lost his parents in the attack on Malaga and had simply drifted around Spain until he had found someone to feed and clothe him. Most Spanish outfits had adopted lost children in this way and they enjoyed a privileged position as a sort of mascot. This 'Manuelino' had been with our neighbours for several months, on different fronts, and appeared almost to have forgotten his home and family. He had a uniform of sorts, plenty of food and everyone was kind to him – his situation was far better than the life of hard work and semi-starvation he would have led on a peasant holding in Andalusia. After the War, many of these children were rounded up for 're-education' and they must have had a pretty horrible time after their days of freedom with the army.

It was at this time of general demoralization at the Front that we got news of the POUM revolt in Barcelona. It was impossible then to discover the truth about these events, but they served to heighten the feeling that the Communists were in control of the situation and that they would exploit it to suit their own advantage without any sort of consideration for anyone but themselves. The POUM was the largest of a number of Marxist organizations which did not subscribe to the official Communist Party line. The official Party now produced a mass of palpably absurd propaganda, claiming that the POUM were in alliance with Franco who, for all his faults, certainly would not have allied himself with a small party of dissident Marxists. It is never comfortable for a soldier to feel that there is a struggle for power amongst the politicians behind the line, but in a civil war, fought on the basis of the 'Popular Front' alliance of anyone opposed to the principle of Fascist dictatorships, it was disastrous. There were the wildest rumours, spread officially and unofficially – the POUM had linked up with Franco supporters in Barcelona to raise a revolt in our rear but had been wiped out by the loyal forces of Party stalwarts defending peace and democracy. At the other extreme, the Party had sprung a plot to annihilate the leaders of all opposition parties in the Popular Front in order to turn the bourgeois Civil War into a Communist revolt. There was no source of information that could be trusted and everyone became uneasy.

The POUM militia, like the Anarchists, had tried to fight the War by democratic process – officers were elected and dismissed by a free vote, day to day tactics were decided by a council of the regiment. Even strategic questions concerning the deployment of the militia were decided in conference. In terms of modern warfare it was all criminally naive, but these were the sort of people who formed the bulk of the army and the industrial manpower backing it up which made it possible for the army to exist. Arrests and executions were not going to change their beliefs and there simply wasn't time enough to re-educate them. The POUM was no worse than many other organizations in this respect but it had many thousands of members and in Catalonia was in a numerically stronger position than the Communist Party itself. In Communist eyes their worst crime was that they claimed to be the official Marxist party of the country. This was heresy, indeed! We were back to a position as bizarre as the Wars of the Monophysite Heresy in the days of Byzantium, when false belief was even more heinous than unbelief.

The events of Barcelona were reflected in the situation within the Brigade. Rumours of men disappearing, of secret trials and executions, increased more than ever before. People started to guard their tongues and to look over their shoulders when they spoke in any critical way of authority. How much truth there was in the rumours, I don't know. André Marty later claimed that he had ordered 'only' 500 executions, but there appears to be plenty of evidence that this was understating the case considerably. In any event, this was not what I had come to Spain for, and I was determined that I should get out at the very first opportunity. It was no longer my war.

One of the inherent defects of the Communist Party is a passion for conspiratorial activity and its corollary of suspicion. Throughout the War the leadership was convinced that among the International Brigades there were a number of people who were Fascists who had joined for the purpose of spying and sabotage. Personally I consider this proposition to be ludicrously improbable. Practically none of them spoke Spanish, without which it would have been absolutely impossible to pass back and forth through the enemy lines, and since Franco had complete mastery of the air, there was very little about our troop movements of which he was not aware. In point of fact, it is extremely unlikely that any man would put his life in jeopardy in order to convey to the enemy the paltry information that the average line soldier is able to collect. There is no doubt that Franco had spies in plenty, but they were Spaniards, and they were employing themselves much more efficiently than they would by sitting around in the trenches of Jarama. The same thing was true of sabotage. The amount of sabotage which an individual soldier in the line can commit is strictly limited by the circumstance of his being confined to a small area. If a man wants to commit effective sabotage he does not join an infantry regiment where he has less privacy than he would enjoy in prison. He can only operate if allowed freedom of movement – as in the case of the partisan fighter. I certainly know of no single instance of planned sabotage during the time that I was in the

7. Soup from the cookhouse reaches the men of the Brigades
   (*Robert Capa*)

8. Going over the top *(Associated Press Photo)*

9. A machine-gun position *(Robert Capa)*

Brigades. There were occasional acts of bloody-mindedness, which might occur in any army, but no man would have enlisted simply in order to commit them.

Now that there was decent weather, and a comparatively safe front, the Communist Party started a regular tourist agency to enable distinguished visitors to view the Front for propaganda purposes. But this parade of notoriety-hunters did very little to boost the flagging morale of the Brigade. Our visitors fell roughly into three classes – the patronizing, the hearty, and those who had the good grace to feel embarrassed. Most of these occasions had something of the character of a Board of Guardians paying their annual visit to an orphanage. They were clean, decently dressed, well fed, and in no real danger, while we were dirty, ragged, hungry and desperately unsure of our future. But above all, we were there to stay, while they only had to put up with the dirt and stink for half an hour – an occasional shot overhead to remind them of the realities provided an extra excitement. Professor Haldane and his wife Charlotte came to inspect us. Cartier-Bresson came and took photographs. Dos Passos, Spender, Auden, MacLeish, Hemingway and others paid us a visit. The most controversial of them all was Ernest Hemingway, full of hearty and bogus *bonhomie*. He sat himself down behind the bullet-proof shield of a machine-gun and loosed off a whole belt of ammunition in the general direction of the enemy. This provoked a mortar bombardment for which he did not stay.

One of the most remarkable visitors was Herbert Mathews, correspondent of the *New York Times*, who looked and behaved like a Yankee banker. He was a tall, thin, angular man, whose clothes hung on him as on a clothes horse, with a long, thin, bony face which always carried a faintly disapproving expression. It was quite an experience to meet Mathews walking through the trenches. He always wore a city suit with a collar and tie, looking as if he had just stepped out of an office. His clothes were rather old-fashioned and he wore the kind of lace-up boots which were the approved footwear for city gents of my grandfather's generation. He was rather coldly treated by the Battalion, who felt that the representative of the arch-conservative *New York Times* must necessarily be antipathetic to our cause. In the event, we were entirely wrong. He strongly supported the Republican side in his paper and wrote fairly and well of us in his book – *The Education of a Corres-*

pondent. We had Clement Attlee and various other stalwarts of the Labour and Trades Union movements. We ran the gamut of the arts from Stephen Spender to Errol Flynn. Every aspiring writer to the left of centre in politics endeavoured to get himself a trip to witness the agonies of the Republic. We were told to be on our best behaviour and avoid any kind of 'negative' remark, but the visitors were always so well surrounded by Political Commissars that there was little danger. Most annoying of the visitors were the type that said, 'God, I wish I was able to stay out here with you fellows' – the implication presumably being that their activities were so important that their presence could not be afforded, while us lucky chaps had the leisure to enjoy the real fun.

The food was becoming steadily worse, and no real attempt was made at cooking, beyond chucking everything available into a tub of water and boiling it. The result was a whitish-looking fluid consisting principally of potatoes and dried beans with occasional vestiges of meat and olive oil. It was cold by the time it got up to the line and usually looked so unappetizing that it was barely worth the effort to eat it. It blotted up your hunger but it gave no joy. Coffee and sugar had disappeared and cigarettes or any form of tobacco were hard to come by. But there was still plenty of drink and my periodic forays through the Battalion sector required terrific stamina as I was constantly invited in for a drink at one dug-out after another. These people were living herded together in a small section of the trench for months on end – they were sick of one another's company, so that having a drink with someone else was a real relief to them. But visiting fifteen or twenty dug-outs meant quite a tremendous intake, always on an empty stomach. Since I was the only person who got out of the line at all regularly, I was the only source of news and information, except the gossip that came up via the cookhouse. This was, in many ways, a dangerous situation. It would only have needed one report from a zealous Communist to the Political Commissar to the effect that I had been saying something out of place and I too would have disappeared from circulation. Fortunately I always managed to keep the conversation light and to enjoy the company of my friends without running foul of the political establishment.

II

Last Days at Jarama

In the midst of so much demoralization and boredom, a rumour began to grow that our Brigade was due to be relieved for rest and reconstruction. We knew that there was a build-up of new recruits around Albecete. There were all sorts of stories about the new Officers' School said to have been started under Merriman, Wintringham and others who had recovered from wounds received at Jarama. And there seemed to be a lot of activity around Brigade HQ which could indicate some sort of re-organization. Finally, orders came through one morning that we were to be relieved that night by the *Quatorzième*, which threw the whole Battalion into a fever of excitement. The French advance party arrived at about four o'clock in the afternoon. Neither Marty nor Steve spoke French, and none of the French spoke English, so it was a complicated business planning our withdrawal by sections from the left and the simultaneous French takeover. The operation was planned for midnight on a completely moonless night. Our machine-guns, with ammunition and spare parts, had to be taken out of their emplacements and worked back through narrow communication trenches, to be replaced by the French. All this had to be carried out in the pitch dark, keeping our movements undiscovered by the enemy who were only about 200 yards away. Our end of the business went ahead quite smoothly as we knew the ground, but the unfortunate French were not so lucky. They made such a hell of a row getting themselves organized in their new positions that they attracted a lot of panic firing and a few mortar bombs from the Fascist trenches, but no serious damage was done.

We trundled all our gear down to the Chinchón road, where we found a fleet of trucks waiting for us. I don't know exactly how long we had been up on Jarama but it seemed like forever, and we had almost given up hope of ever getting out of the damned place. Finally the trucks got under way: we didn't know where we were going and we didn't care, as long as it was away from the Jarama Front. The convoy of trucks appeared to wander around all over central Spain with long halts for no apparent reason, and it was evening before we arrived at Alcalá de Henares, only about 75 miles from our starting point. Billets had been arranged all along one side of the street facing the main square.

The Battalion HQ billet had real beds, such as I hadn't seen for many months. Marty and I dumped our louse-infested clothing in the passage, and had a glorious shower with soap in cold water, before going to bed in coarse but clean sheets. It was like a foretaste of paradise. We had a room to ourselves and I put up a 'Do not disturb' notice on the door. We did not move again until ten o'clock the following morning. The old lady who owned the house had washed and ironed our clothing during the night. She produced two large mugs of the peculiar tasting chocolate which the Spaniards love, with two hunks of bread, fresh from the oven. We shaved and bathed again and felt ready for anything.

All the billets were in one street and when we went out into the sunshine it looked like the aftermath of a bubonic plague. There were men lying all over the sidewalk, and propped up against the walls, sleeping or shouting, half-dressed, some of them lying in pools of their own vomit and generally in the most deplorable conditions. Practically the entire Battalion, or what there was left of it, was blind, paralytic drunk. This was precisely what I had done myself the first time I had got out of the line on one of my trips: consequently I did not feel in the mood to blame anybody, but it was a pretty depressing sight. Anybody who did not know what they had been through would have written them off as a worthless bunch of layabouts. It would have been so damned easy.

Marty and I decided to leave them to it and let them sober up in their own time. The town looked dirty and dilapidated. It was only a few miles behind the line and most of the local inhabitants appeared to have cleared out and left it. There was nothing to buy in the few shops which were left open and the streets were almost entirely deserted. We had only been strolling around for about half an hour when a motor-cycle drew up alongside of us with a message from Brigade HQ. We had orders to be prepared to move at 20.00 hours and return to our old trench line at Jarama.

It was unbelievable.

The despatch rider stormed away on his bike and left Marty with the signal in his hand. For some appreciable time he stood and cursed, fluently and methodically. He cursed the entire leadership of the International Brigades and all their forbears. He cursed the uncaring stupidity of their minds and their total lack of sensibility. It was quite a performance but at least he got the whole thing out of his system instead of leaving it to rankle. 'I don't look forward to tell the guys about this. They'll go raving mad.'

'And you can't blame them, I know how I feel myself.'

'I don't blame them. But they've got to be told.'

'Why don't you let the Political bloke do it? That's what he's supposed to be there for.'

'By Jesus I'd certainly like to but then they'd go mad all together.'

'Why don't you try and get on to Copic and see if you can get the order held up for a day or two?'

'It's no use, Pat. The whole ballsup comes from somewhere much higher up the line than Copic. We'll have to go back to that stinking Jarama whether we like it or not.'

'It begins to look as if we'll never get out of it.'

'Ah well, stuff it. Let's go and have a drink.'

When we got back to the street where the billets were, we found that the grapevine had been working as efficiently as ever and everyone knew that we were headed back for Jarama. I never discovered how the news leaked out unless it was from the despatch rider. Fortunately the big booze-up had deflated the capacity for anger, and although there was a considerable amount of mutinous talk there was no absolute refusal to obey orders. But it was a very angry bunch of men that piled into the trucks that evening.

Back in the trenches, things were even worse than before. In only twenty-four hours the *Quatorzième* had turned the place into a pig-sty. They had used the dug-outs as latrines, and broken food, bottles and tins were scattered all over the place. It was several days before we got the place clean again. The dirt and stink produced by the French did have one peculiar benefit: our beefing was no longer restricted to Copic and the Brigade staff; we could now curse the French, which made a pleasant change. Nobody ever took the trouble to explain the crazy muddle that had taken us up to Alcala and back, all in twenty-four hours, and I never discovered any reason for it. But certainly it did nothing to build up confidence in the leadership.

After this pathetic piece of bungling, life returned to the pattern we had come to regard as normality – stand-to at first light in the morning, breakfast of sorts, CO's inspection, cleaning guns, digging and filling latrine trenches, midday meal, evening stand-to, evening meal, night-patrols. The only forms of recreation were poker, black-jack or drink. We were provided with no reading matter apart from propaganda leaflets, and the few books we did have had been read too often. Candles were very scarce so that most people had nothing to do at night but to sit chatting in the dark or to try to sleep, without the benefit of pillow or mattress, with only one blanket, and the lice as constant companions. Everybody was tired, dirty, bored and dispirited. With the improvement in the weather there was a lot of dysentery which was not severe enough to justify hospital treatment and a break from the line, and only served to make life all the more depressing.

Somebody wrote:

> *There's a valley in Spain called Jarama,*
> *That's a place that we all know so well,*
> *For 'tis here that we wasted our manhood,*
> *And most of our old age as well.*
>
> *From this valley they tell us we're leaving,*
> *But don't hasten to bid us adieu,*
> *For ee'n though we make our departure,*
> *We'll be back in an hour or two.*
>
> *Oh we're proud of our Lincoln Battalion,*
> *And the marathon record it's made,*
> *Please do us this little favour,*
> *And take this last word to Brigade.*
>
> *You'll never be happy with strangers,*
> *They would not understand you as we,*
> *So remember the Jarama Valley,*
> *And the old men who wait patiently.*

This, with variations, was sung to the tune of 'The Red River Valley' and was particularly favoured to bait Political Commissars. The tragic part of the situation was that the vast majority of us still felt convinced of the justice of our cause and were anxious to fight for it, which only increased our sense of frustration.

One of the most depressing aspects of my life at this time was my early morning trip down to Brigade HQ. The safest route was by the winding road along which supplies were brought up to the Front. There was a short cut across the hills, but there was always a fair amount of spent shot whistling around and it seemed rather stupid to run the risk of being knocked off by a bullet that had been fired miles away and had certainly never been aimed at me. The only disadvantage of the road was that it took me through the 'meat yard' which had been quarried out to a level that placed it below the line of any direct fire. The 'meat yard' was used as a temporary storage area and as a place for the trucks to turn and unload. It was here that the day's quota of corpses were deposited while awaiting removal. The numbers varied between two and twenty. Snipers and mortar fire took a small but regular toll, and every morning a number of these utterly forlorn objects were laid out there under their blankets. Nothing looks deader than a dead man, particularly the positions of the feet which look exactly like those of a marionette when released from the strings of its controller. The dead were as utterly meaningless as discarded banana skins, and that was the fact which particularly depressed me.

The Christian teaching to which I had been subjected as a child had never really meant anything to me, but until now I had supported a vague belief in life after death. I imagine that the wish was both father and mother to the thought. But even this belief now became ridiculous – the dead looked so utterly and irrevocably dead that it was impossible to imagine that any part of them had survived. All my childhood teaching had been heavily coloured by the idea of earthly sin and divine punishment after death. I don't know that I had ever believed it, but had merely accepted the whole concept without analysis. Now, however, the whole structure of morality, as I had unthinkingly accepted it, had entirely collapsed. If there was no after life there was no basis for traditional morality.

This may not have been a very original piece of thinking, but for me it was quite devastating. I had grown up in the English middle-class tradition of the period which was seriously concerned with right and wrong, with good and evil, with what was proper and improper, but this moral code had to have some basis of justification. I had never believed in the Anglican Christ – it was too palpably a convenient fiction for supporting the Empire and the Establishment – but I had vaguely accepted a notion of the 'supreme being' which I had never bothered to define, simply out of intellectual laziness. I had acquiesced to a number of vague fictions to save myself the trouble of having to think about them. I wasn't an intellectual, I was an artist, concerned almost entirely with emotional and sensual criteria. The loss of my intellectual props was a serious one. I had been under severe strain for several months. The nobility of the cause for which I had come to Spain was clearly a fiction, and now the sudden and absolute conviction that life was an experience with no past and no future, merely ending in annihilation, left me in dire confusion and it was while I was in this condition that I received the wound that put an end to my military career.

Meanwhile, on another level, life went on fairly happily for me personally. I had a great number of friends with whom I was very happy. The weather was beautiful and I was developing the soldier's knack of closing my mind to the things that I did not care to think about. I was busy enough to keep myself interested and things in general were not too bad. But it was too good to be true for long.

One morning a message had arrived from Brigade HQ that all Battalion Commanders and Commissars were to report back for a conference. I was sitting in the dug-out when Marty and Steve returned from it.

'That fucking Copic', said Marty, as he sat down. Steven Nelson sat on the other side, looking equally despondent.

'What's he up to this time?' I asked.

'Comrade, we are about to make a great attack and drive the Fascist hordes back across the Jarama river.'

'Us and who else?'

'It's no use going on like this, Marty,' Steve chimed in. 'These are the orders and we're stuck with it.'

'I know we're stuck with it, but all this crap about tanks and aircraft and artillery and the *Pasionaria* Brigade is bullshit, like it was in February, and you know it. There's no sign of any of that support.'

'There must be some good reason for its non-appearance and we shall simply have to do what we can.'

'If there is a reason, then for Christ's sake why doesn't he tell us what the hell it is?'

'We have to preserve security, Comrade.'

'O.K., Comrade, we have to preserve security. So am I going hoofing across the lines to tell Franco why we're pretending to make a damn-fool pretence of an attack? I don't get it. However, if Copic wants an attack I suppose he'll have to get it but I warn you – I'm not going to give any orders to the Battalion to climb out of the trench and get themselves slaughtered until there is some real support.'

Steve Nelson didn't like it, but he wisely kept quiet because he knew damned well that if things turned out as he expected, the entire Battalion was sufficiently angry to mutiny, as it had done before. It was the same story as the 27th February when the promised planes, artillery and tanks had never turned up, and 80 per cent of the Battalion had been destroyed.

Company and Platoon Commanders were summoned to the Battalion HQ and Marty gave them the official story. He did his best to try and present it as if he believed in it, but it did not sound very convincing. In theory, the troops on our left flank were to be reinforced by the Lister Brigade – one of the best of the Spanish assault forces – and they, together with the *Pasionaria* Brigade, were to make the break-through, supported by our Brigade on their right flank. There was to be an intense aerial bombardment of the enemy lines to our front, opening at dawn, followed by an artillery barrage, opening at 08.00 hours. The combined Lister and *Pasionaria* Brigades, supported by a considerable force of tanks, would go over the top at 09.00 hours, followed by ourselves. It all sounded very fine and nobody believed a word of it. Steve did his best to try and reassure us that this time it was all going to be different. He did his best to infer that our effort was no more than a diversion to distract the enemy from far more important and far-reaching events which would vitally affect the whole progress of the War. The impression was that we should meet very little resistance and the whole thing would be a hayride. It was a virtuoso performance that might have succeeded if there had been more visible indications that we would receive our backing support. But the gossip which came up from the cookhouse told of no signs of activity in our rear, and the boys had become completely distrustful of any statement which emanated from Copic.

The Company and Platoon Commanders rejoined their units and explained the situation to their men. During the afternoon I went up to the front trench line to arrange my observation post and telephone line. I found everyone roaring with laughter.

'Have you heard the news, Comrade? We are about to make a glorious attack.'

'Yes indeed, Comrade. The aviation will destroy the enemy's line at sunrise.'

'It'll be the first time that we've seen any planes on this front.'

'Ah, but, Comrade, this time it is going to be different.'

'Yes, Comrade, this time it is going to be entirely different.'

'And the massed artillery will lay down a barrage of tremendous power.'

'I haven't seen any artillery.'

'But you will, Comrade. This will be supported by a considerable force of tanks.'

'Well, by Jesus, I hope you're right.'

'We must have faith in our glorious revolutionary leadership.'

'Copic?'

'Yes, Comrade. Our glorious leader, the Comrade Brigade Commander Copic, has given his personal assurance. Our advance will be irresistible.'

But beneath all the nonsense there was a rather sinister feeling of impending disaster. My own duties constantly took me down to Brigade HQ and the area behind the lines so that I knew that there was no build-up for an offensive. I kept my own counsel, but could see no reason for all this pantomime. Our Brigade had about five hundred men to hold approximately four kilometres of line. The enemy trenches were about two hundred yards away and any attempt which we might make to advance across this area in the face of considerable machine-gun fire would obviously be disastrous. However, we spent the day going through the motions of preparing for an attack. During the night I had fixed up a very strong observation post at the head of a sap from which I could see the whole of no-man's land for about a thousand yards in both directions, as well as the enemy front line. It was constructed of steel rails with a half-inch slot between them and a heavy cover of sandbags, which gave the maximum field of vision with a theoretical margin of safety.

Marty and I were awake practically all night. We did not talk about the situation, although we both knew what the other thought. Finally we breakfasted on a couple of dry bread rolls and hot coffee with a lacing of brandy, wished one another good luck, and I went off to my observation post. I was joined by a Polish-American sergeant, Dave Polansky, who was appointed to act as my runner if the telephone lines were blown out. There had been no sign of any troop movements over on the left flank and I was convinced that the famous Brigades who were supposed to initiate the advance were a myth. Some reinforcements had been brought up into their lines on the day before, but they were certainly not of Brigade strength and they did not have the appearance or the equipment of a crack assault force.

As the sun came up over the horizon, the day was beautifully crisp and clear. There was no sign of any bombing or artillery, which surprised no one. Someone brought us up a couple of mugs of coffee and we sat down to smoke and relax. We'd never fully believed in the attack but we had been all tensed up in case it really should happen. Dave was normally rather laconic by nature and mistrusted any speech that did not have a positive purpose, but in the emotional let-down he became quite talkative.

'You know Pat, I don't figure these guys', he nodded his head in the direction of the *Pasionaria* Brigade. 'In the early days they must have fought like bastards. They had the whole Spanish army against them and they managed to hold on – now they don't seem to give a damn.'

'It's pretty hard to keep white hot all the time.'

'It's not that. You take that Brigade alongside of us here – they're supposed to be one of the crack outfits, but look at them. They've got the look of men that are just waiting to get beaten. They've taken such a beating for so long that they can't any longer believe it's their turn to win.'

'They don't have to lose, for Christ's sake. There's arms and tanks and planes coming in from Russia. There are still men pouring in to join the IBs.'

'They hate our guts, Pat. Don't you know that? They hate to need us. They're Spanish, so how would you like to call in another guy to help beat the hell out of your old man.'

By nine o'clock there was rather heavier rifle and machine-gun fire than usual but, apart from that, everything was perfectly normal. It was not until eleven o'clock that our three old pieces of artillery started to bang off a few desultory rounds. But the artillery had no observer up in the line and all their fire went wailing over our heads to fall far away behind the enemy lines. As preparation for our projected offensive it was completely ineffectual. However, this was the moment that Copic selected to order us over the top into no man's land. He insisted that the *Pasionaria* had moved out and that we must follow them in support.

Marty rang through to me. 'Brigade say that the *Pasionarias* are already well out into no-man's-land. Why the hell haven't you let me know?'

'Look, Marty, I don't care what Brigade say. I can see the whole of their lines for a thousand yards and more. There is no sign of any advance and you can hear for yourself that there is not even any heavy firing.'

'You are absolutely sure that no one has moved out?'

'Sure, I'm sure. No bastard can move down there without me seeing them. I'm looking right down over their lines and there's no sign of movement.'

'You realize that this is my neck. I've told Copic that I won't move the Battalion out without support. If they have moved and I don't, he'll have me – sure as God.'

'Then send up Steve Nelson to take a look for himself and report back to Copic. He's bound to believe his own Political Commissar.'

Steve came up and did his best to see all sorts of activity where Copic said it was, but even he had to admit that there was no sign of movement. Finally he went back and reported to Copic. Marty was in a particularly dangerous position as a non-Communist. At the Brigade conference he had insisted that he would not order the Battalion over the top without support. If he did so now, and they were carved up, he would carry the blame. On the other hand, he was refusing a direct order from the Brigade Commander and that was going to be a pretty difficult thing to get away with. The probability is that the Divisional Commander was playing the two Brigades off, one against the other, by bluffing both that one of us had advanced and the other must support, in the hope of getting some sort of movement somewhere. The only strength in Marty's position was the certainty that the entire Battalion, including the Political Commissars, would support him. But even this would not help in the event of a trial by Party officials in the neurotic atmosphere of Albacete.

This situation continued for a couple of hours; Copic continually on the phone to Marty insisting that the *Pasionarias* had gone over and that we must support them, backed up with threats of court-martials and firing squads. In the midst of all this clamour, three Russian tanks appeared in the dead ground to the rear of the English lines. These were nothing like the monsters which we became used to during the Second World War. They only moved at about 10 m.p.h. and carried a rapid firing cannon, firing a small shell of about two pounds, and a machine-gun. This small element of support was unlikely to play a very decisive part in the action, but Marty felt that he could no longer resist the order to advance. He went through the lines trying to stir up some enthusiasm and giving his orders to Company and Platoon officers. The tanks waddled up and crossed the English lines, firing as they went. Marty gave the signal and the Battalion started to go over the top.

My position was ahead of the line of advance and almost at the extreme left of the Battalion sector, so that I was in a position to oversee the whole movement. Marty, the Flaherty brothers, and Paul Burn burst out from the centre of the line with a bunch of about twenty-five others. Further up to the right there was another group of about the same number, but it was too far away to distinguish any individuals. To my left was Ray, the cynic of the Battalion, at the head of another group. After a short interval, individuals and small parties of men began to emerge somewhat reluctantly and most of them did not go far before diving for any available cover. The original 'wave' ran like hell until they reached the sunken road about 75 yards out. I saw a number of men hit and remain lying where they fell. There was a certain amount of move-ment from the British on our right, but they only had 120 men in the whole thousand yards of their sector and it was perfectly obvious that they could not do very much if they did succeed in crossing the couple of hundred yards to the enemy lines. The Spanish to our left kept up a tremendous fusillade of rifle and machine-gun fire, but only a small group of about a dozen on our immediate flank went over the top. The tanks moved slowly forward, firing as they went. But they had only advanced about 75 yards when one of them stopped – apparently disabled – and the other two retired as fast as they could go back over the British lines into dead ground, and were never seen again. The enemy were blazing away with everything they had, long after every visible target had disappeared.

While the firing was at its height I heard a great gasp from Dave and turned round to see what was the matter with him. The only thing wrong that I could see as he turned round to face me was what appeared to be a black mark in the centre of his forehead. He never said anything, but I have never seen such a look of total surprise on a human face. There was no expression of pain or sadness, or anything else other than pure surprise, in that instant as he stood looking at me before he dropped to the ground, stone dead. He had been hit by the million to one chance of a bullet passing through the half-inch slot between the two steel rails of the observation defence. There was no use calling for stretcher bearers, so I forced myself to turn back to my job. Dave Polansky was dead – there hadn't been anything extraordinary about him. He was just an ordinary working-class Polish-American from some industrial city in the mid-West. There was nothing high-flown or idealistic about him. Born in a slum, educated in an over-crowded State school, gone to work in a series of underpaid, boring jobs in between spells of un-employment. He wasn't a Communist or a member of any political organization, but he had believed in justice as he saw it and for that he had died. He now lies in an unmarked grave somewhere up in the Jarama hills, nobody knows where, and I don't suppose anyone cares. Just one of hundred of millions killed in all the untold numbers of wars since the world began.

From my position I could see a number of men on either side who appeared to be dead. Several more, obviously wounded, were struggling around trying to look after their wounds or to find some cover where they could lie up till nightfall. One body appeared to be burning quite fiercely and, in fact, the red glow of the burning corpse could be seen for several nights. What caused this I have no idea, but it was all pretty horrible. I could see the men in the sunken road, out in no-man's-land.

Some were wounded, but as they were about four feet below ground level they were in no further danger. The massive small-arms fire continued with unabated rage long after any target, except the stranded tank, had disappeared. I sat there in silent rage at the waste and stupidity of the whole affair, for it was perfectly obvious that we could not put a sufficient number of men across to achieve any useful purpose. Those who had been killed and wounded had suffered to achieve no useful purpose whatsoever.

Marty and Steve were, of course, out in the sunken road and out of communication so, after I had cooled down a bit, I went back to the Battalion HQ dug-out to report back to Brigade. I met a number of men who had failed to go over the top. They all looked a trifle shamefaced and anxious to give themselves some sort of an alibi. I didn't blame them, but I was in no mood to talk about it. I got on the phone to one of the Russian interpreters and gave my report. After a few moments Copic came on the phone in person. He raved and shouted in half a dozen different languages. He refused to believe that the *Pasionaria* had not moved, he abused British and Americans indiscriminately, he abused me personally; but it was all in vain. The whole show was a complete flop as he should have known it would be. I went over to Doc Pike's dug-out dressing station. He had about half-a-dozen patients who had been hit as they went over the top, and had either fallen or been dragged back into the trench. Most of them had been fixed up as far as he could manage with the small resources available and were waiting to be carried down to the meat yard, ready for the ambulance, but three were already dead. They were all friends of a couple of months' standing, and the sight of them lying dead and wounded behind the dug-out made me feel very sick indeed. I was obsessed with the idea that I ought to do something about it, but there wasn't a damn thing that I could do. The doc had finished his work for the moment and took me down into the dug-out for a large brandy. I told him about the whole show and warned him to expect at least twenty more patients as soon as darkness fell, and we were able to get in the rest of them. He was so admirably cool and sensible about the whole thing that I began to feel better.

There was nothing to do until dark but the danger was that those left in the trenches might panic at the considerable movement in no-man's-land and start blazing away at a supposed counter-attack before we could get the wounded back into the trench. The machine-gun crews were all intact in their position within the trench, as the plan had provided for their forward movement only after the enemy trench was secured. Consequently we had one Company Commander and half-a-dozen petty officers in the trench to control the situation. All firing from our side had ceased completely, for fear of hitting anyone in the forward area, and gradually the enemy fire died away to a fairly normal sniping fire. The only thing now was to wait for darkness – and a very distressing period of waiting it was.

As darkness increased, one or two of the men who had been wounded close to the trench dragged themselves or stumbled back. The machine-gunners went out in pairs to look for dead or wounded and finally the uninjured men from the sunken road, some of them carrying a wounded comrade on their backs, filtered back. Periodically, one of the enemy machine-guns would open up, but it was too dark for them to find a specific target and no harm was done. The ones that did return were all dying of thirst: it had been a long, hot day and they had had no water bottles with them. There is nothing that dries a man's mouth worse than lying out for hours with insufficient cover and the bullets ripping through the air, just over his head.

Everyone was raging against Copic, and the Brigade staff. Meetings were being held all along the line; the men were threatening to march out of the trenches and the Political Commissars trying to give out soothing words. Fortunately, everyone was too tired to take any serious action, and the reaction from the day's tension resulted in everybody talking at once but not doing very much. Nobody blamed Marty as they knew that he had stuck out his own neck as long as possible on behalf of the Battalion, but if Copic had showed his face there would have been quite an ugly scene. The casualties had not been as bad as they might have been owing to the presence of the sunken road. The men had gone over the top with no real determination, and as soon as good cover presented itself, they had dived in and stayed put. The enemy troops on the other side were no more than a holding force of second-rate infantry who produced a tremendous fusillade, but apart from a few snipers, their fire was very inaccurate.

This attack could never possibly have been successful. We were too

10.
War damage in the villages *(United Press International)*

11.
The way back *(Robert Capa)*

12. The final stand-down parade *(Robert Capa)*

thin on the ground – approximately one man to every five metres of trench to storm the enemy line even if we had been able to cross the intervening no-man's-land without casualties. It was impossible to estimate the enemy's available numbers, though they were probably no greater than our own. But they were well supplied with automatic weapons, and were firing from fortified positions against an attack which would be forced to cross some two hundred yards with no cover and with no light-automatic weapons. As soon as our men moved out of the trenches our heavy machine-guns were unable to fire without killing our own men. This was the position, and the vast majority of the men were well aware of it. They were perfectly willing to fight, but not to set themselves up to be slaughtered in an enterprise which had no hope of success from the outset. The preparatory bombardment which we had been promised had not taken place and when the order came to go over the top, a number of the men simply remained where they were. No explanation of this disastrous farce was ever forthcoming, and it is only now that I can discern any possible reason for it. Franco's offensive against the Basque provinces opened on 31st March and it is possible that this was a diversionary attack, but if so, why did nobody tell us either before or afterwards and why were we told so many lies? Copic continued to persist in the story that an advance had been made by the Brigades on our left, in spite of the fact that we could see with our own eyes that it was not so. However, it had become dangerous by this time to insist that White was White if the leadership maintained that it was Black. We had reached the position where individuals suddenly disappeared from circulation and it was unwise to ask about their whereabouts.

I was by now heartily sick of the whole affair and busy looking for an opportunity to get out of the whole show. I wasn't prepared to desert from the trenches but I was determined to seize the chance if the day ever came when we were given the leave which had been so often promised. Apart from our one night at Alcalá, we had been continuously on duty for three months and had been in the line for a particularly bloody two months. What distressed me most was the continuous spate of false propaganda and lies, and the incompetence. Above all was the knowledge that we were being used to make a political point and not to try and win a war. I was prepared to be killed fighting to achieve a form of social justice for Spain, but not to achieve a talking point for the Communist Party or anybody else.

There was a small road menders' hut at the junction of the San Martín-Morata road with that leading to Chinchón. The road junction itself was quite a dangerous place to hang about in as there was quite a lot of stray shot reaching it from the front, which lay about 1,500 yards ahead and two hundred feet above it. The road menders' hut on the other hand was protected by a shoulder of the hill and was perfectly safe, so that it had become a general meeting place, for all of us who had reason to be moving around behind the line – supply parties, ambulances, despatch riders, observers or anybody who found some pretext to get out of the trenches for an hour or so. It was the only place in the whole area where one felt entirely safe from the enemy and free of officialdom. I frequently stopped in there for a cigarette and a chat on my way back and forth between the Battalion and Brigade HQ. One day I was standing by the door chatting with Giles Romilly when a strange ambulance pulled up and the driver got out. He was not wearing any particular kind of uniform, but from his dress he was obviously American.

'I shouldn't stand around over there,' I called. 'A guy got hit there only this morning.' So he came over and joined us at the hut. And this was how I ran into another Ray, the driver of an ambulance from the American Hospital, whose appearance was to radically alter the whole pattern of my life,

'Thanks for the tip. There seemed to be a hell of a lot of crap whistling around there but I reckoned it was all too high to be dangerous.'

'Most of it is, but you can't bet on it. What're you doing up here?'

'I'm looking for a guy in the Lincoln Battalion. Do you know where I can find them?'

'Sure I do. Who are you looking for?'

'A guy called Pat Gurney. I've got some stuff for him.'

'Well, I've saved you a trip. I'm Pat Gurney.'

'Jesus, that's a piece of luck. I'll get the stuff.' He ran across the road and came back with several letters and a parcel. 'Freddy Martin, she's the matron of the American Hospital, sent me over to find you. She brought these from your girl-friend in New York.'

'Thanks a lot.' There was a parcel of real cigarettes, candies, razor blades, cans of coffee, and all the things which we most needed. I have never seen such a cornucopia of a parcel. There were letters from Evelyn, an American girl I had known in Paris, and a very sweet letter from Freddy asking me to come over and visit them at the American Hospital, if only for a single night. This was my first real contact with the world of normality for several months, and it made a new man out of me. The ambulance driver accepted a cigarette and wished me well. 'I must get back now, this is a fairly unofficial trip. My name's Ray. It was nice to meet you and I hope I see you again.' He dashed back to his ambulance and shot off down the road to Morata.

During the previous summer I had spent about two months with Evelyn after meeting her in the Dome in Paris. We had been very much in love and very happy, but circumstances had compelled her return to New York in September. She had a husband and two children and not being much of a letter writer, I had, more or less written the whole thing off. However, she had heard from mutual friends in Paris that I was in the Brigades so that when Freddy, who was a friend of hers, left New York for Spain, Evelyn had loaded her up with letters and presents for me. Up to that point I had received no communication from anyone outside Spain. I had felt completely cut off from my previous way of life but had experienced no real sense of loss. Spain for me was a world of nightmare that had no relationship with the real world. Before I came to Spain my chief interests in life had been sex, sculpture, drink and good company, but from the moment that I left London I had hardly thought of women or my trade, which, looking back on it, was pretty extraordinary. I was no political fanatic, I hadn't 'seen the light' or anything of that sort, but for some reason which I am quite unable to understand, I had become a totally different person – sober and chaste and somewhat withdrawn. However this brush with the outside world suddenly put me back into contact with my natural self. Amongst the letters was a note from Freddy (for Frederika) suggesting that I try and get a night away from the front and come down to the hospital for a break.

This appeared to me as an absolutely fabulous notion. I had come to identify myself with the Battalion so completely that it had not occurred to me that I could have any action, apart from it. The idea of spending an evening in female company, having a bath, and sleeping in sheets, seemed almost too impossibly remote to be real. I should only be out of the line for one night, and since the American Hospital was at that time only about five miles behind our lines, I would hear the noise of the firing if any panic broke out and be able to get a lift back within a short time on one of the ambulances going up to the line.

I felt rather mean when I put the proposition up to Marty, but he simply laughed like hell and wished me luck. So a couple of nights later I rode back on a supply truck that dropped me at the hospital. Suddenly, I felt terribly embarrassed. I knew that this was a world in which I didn't belong. Nurses and orderlies were moving around immaculately dressed in shining white uniforms and everything looked utterly different from the world from which I had just emerged like a spectre. Finally I plucked up my courage and went in to present myself. I was immediately engulfed in American hospitality. When I explained about the condition of my clothes, they were immediately whisked away to be washed and sterilized. I was shown to a bathroom, given clean pyjamas and dressing gown, and left to revel in hot water and soap. When I emerged Freddy and half-a-dozen American nurses were in the recreation room with a huge demi-john of anis. It was heaven.

I just sank back into a glorious euphoria of cleanliness, drink, hot food and female company. I have no distinct recollection of the remainder of the evening. Freddy was infinitely kind and gentle with me. I was woken up in the morning, given coffee, and got dressed in my freshly washed and ironed clothing. So, desperately hung-over but happy, I returned to the Battalion.

It was a strange thing that ever since I had left London I had not thought of women at all, except for a mild flutter with Angelita in Madrigueras which had been more sentimental than sexual. My whole life had been involved with women. They were the most wonderful things in the world for me ever since I had left school, but for the last few months, I hadn't even thought about them. Now everything was different, and my dedication to a soldier's life, fighting for the good cause, fell away. We weren't helping anyone by sitting around on the Jarama hills being gradually whittled away by snipers and dysentery. I didn't like fighting, though I was prepared to have another go at it if anybody wanted me to. But powerless inaction was futile.

As it happened, the whole problem was solved for me quite simply on a fine summer's morning.

During all the months up on Jarama our skeleton Battalion had received no reinforcements, only some members of the original strength, returning from hospital or from a spell in the Penal Battalion. But we had heard recently that a large number of men had arrived from Canada and the States, and were in training around Albacete. This was exciting news because the rumour was that we were to form a new Brigade of two Canadian and two American Battalions – in one of which we were to be included – all under the command of George Nathan. We felt that under these conditions we should make a lot more sense. We would be free of Copic and under a Brigadier who we could really trust, and there would be one language throughout the Brigade so that we would all really understand what everyone was talking about for a change. Officially I belonged to the Brigade staff, and was not a member of the Lincolns, however, I was determined to stay where I was, and Marty agreed that if we were taken out of the XVth Brigade he would arrange my official transfer to the Lincolns. We had shared a dug-out for some three months and, for lack of an adjutant, I had become a sort of unofficial general amanuensis, in which role I had become accepted by the rest of the Battalion. Marty, in his role of Commander, inevitably lived a rather lonely life; he had to maintain absolute neutrality without any close friendships or favourites, but he was by nature a gregarious man and the friendship which we had formed for one another was very strong. He had a terrific sense of humour and, although he had little formal education, a very good mind and a superb sense of human sympathy. He never bore grudges or carried on feuds, he could be tough as hell in public, but there was much more of sorrow for human weakness than condemnation of wickedness in his outlook.

We both realized that when the day finally came for the withdrawal from Jarama and the formation of the new Brigade, we would be faced with a hell of a lot of problems and hard work, but we enjoyed one another's company and worked well together so it wouldn't be too bad. However it was at this stage that our plans were – quite literally – knocked on the head.

12

Hospital and After

On that summer's morning we had just finished a lunch which had been a little less frightful than usual. It was a lovely day and the enemy appeared to be completely quiescent. There was no noise except the vague murmuring buzz of insect life. The Brigade telephone rang with orders from the abominable Bee to obtain a new set of bearings for all the enemy machine-guns in our sector. I knew that this was a completely worthless operation since they were already charted as accurately as they ever would be, and nothing had changed for several weeks. However, I took up my compass and note book, and started work from the junction of our sector with the British Battalion on the right flank. I was in no hurry and stopped off to gossip with friends in various dug-outs as I worked my way along the trench. There was no firing from either side, the vines and the flowers were flowering very prettily in no-man's-land; I was possessed of a particularly happy and carefree attitude towards life in general. I set up the compass at intervals in the small firing-holes in the parapet, my hand held over the glass against the possibility of any reflection from the sun which would reveal my position to the enemy, noted down the bearing and moved on.

I had almost completed the job when I reached an area where the *parados* (the earth banking at the back of the trench) was lower than the parapet. This made it possible for an enemy sniper to see the sky through one of our firing holes – when his view of the sky disappeared he knew that he had a target to set up for him. However the range was over two hundred yards and the firing hole was only about five inches square, so it needed a very fine marksman to score a bull's eye. I had spoken to the Company Commander about it a couple of days before but things were so quiet that nobody had bothered to do anything about it. In my light-hearted mood I never noticed that I was setting up my compass in the exact position where this situation existed. I was moving along the trench peering through the firing holes, one by one, looking for a place where I could get a clear field of vision. Finally I found the place I wanted for a back-bearing, set up my compass and bent down, with my right hand over the top of it, to get the reading.

Suddenly I felt as if there had been an enormous explosion in the centre of my brain. I was not conscious of any pain and as I fell to the ground I remember thinking, quite calmly, 'Christ, I wonder if it's killed me?' No fear, no drama, but a completely detached curiosity. I had been hit by an explosive bullet in the outer side of my right hand which had laid it open for about two and a half inches through the flesh, and left a hole large enough to take a hen's egg. My hand had been pressed against my forehead and the explosion in the middle of my hand had knocked me out, many of the splinters had passed through into my face, and my eyes were damaged. When I came to in Doc Pike's dug-out dressing station, the pain in my hand was tremendous, but what upset me far more was the pain in my eyes. The doctor had dressed my hand and filled me up with morphine which, combined with the concussion, had evidently left me a little mad. Marty was in the dug-out and spoke to me. I was practically in tears, not at my own plight, but obsessed with the idea that I had failed Marty by getting myself shot, just when he needed to make use of me. The morphine injection didn't seem to ease the pain at all but made me feel as if I wanted to vomit. Finally I was carried off to an ambulance and carted off to the field clearance hospital at Colmenar.

Probably the worst experience that any soldier has to face is the ambulance ride to hospital after he is wounded. It is in the nature of things that the road immediately behind the line is in an appalling condition so that the unfortunate passenger is thrown all over the place. He is usually in a condition of severe shock and considerable pain. I was lucky – I had been hit on a quiet day, so I was not kept for hours at the field-dressing station, as usually happened during a major engagement, and I was the sole occupant of the ambulance. Later, I was to see ambulances coming down from the big attack at Brunete, usually with six stretcher cases and two to four walking wounded, after a drive of sixty miles. Men with appalling wounds, which were only roughly dressed, some of whom had been pitched out of their stretchers on to the floor and were already dead. The appalling stench, and the whole place a welter of blood and vomit. It is the nearest thing to hell that I can possibly imagine.

The Spanish Battalion on our left also used the meat yard for their ambulances and supplies as there was no other approach road in their sector and it so happened that the only ambulance available when I was hit belonged to them. The fellows who carried me down tried to explain to the Spanish driver that I should be taken to the American Hospital, but either he did not understand, or could not be bothered, and he took me to the Spanish hospital belonging to his own Brigade. Some of these Spanish hospitals were extremely primitive and although the staff did their best, they did not have either the equipment or the trained personnel which existed in the American set-up. At the time I neither knew or cared where I was taken. I was vaguely aware of voices talking in a foreign language as they prepared me for the operating theatre, but all I cared about was breathing long and deeply at the anaesthetic to put me out of my misery.

I did not wake up until the following morning, to find myself in a pretty lamentable condition. My right hand appeared to be done up in a mass of dressings about the size of a boxing glove and felt like one great ball of pain. My face was also covered in dressings so that I could not see, but at least the pain had gone out of my eyes. My left thumb was afflicted with something that felt like severe pins and needles, and didn't function at all. I appeared to be in quite a mess.

Eventually a Spanish nurse realized that I was awake and came to speak to me. I was still completely dazed and found the greatest difficulty in speaking or understanding Spanish. However she was very sweet and sympathetic which helped a lot. Finally a Czech doctor arrived. He spoke English and radiated optimism. The bandages were rolled off my face and I found that I was able to see. Apparently a number of fragments from the explosive bullet had gone through my hand into my face, but they had managed to extract them and there was no serious injury. A large piece of the bullet had embedded itself in my left bicep and affected the nerve of my left thumb. This, he assured me, would correct itself in time, although a peculiar numbness has remained to the present day. There remained my right hand, and this was hell. After the operation to remove as many pieces of metal as possible, they had packed the cavity with a yard and a half of iodoform gauze tape and sewed up the wound with a couple of inches of the tape projecting. When they took the dressings off, it didn't look like a hand at all, just a huge shapeless mass of flesh with only the thumb and two fingers visible, the sight of which horrified me. The doctor then proceeded to draw out the tape. It was the most exquisite agony imaginable until, mercifully, I passed out. This procedure left me utterly exhausted and I slept for the next twenty-four hours.

When I next awoke the morphine and shock had drained out of me. I was perfectly sane and rational again. I now began to realize how lucky I was – the bullet which should have hit me in the head had exploded in my hand. My eyesight was going to recover, but the injury to my hand meant that I should have no further value as a soldier and should be out of the whole mess. Even if I had no future as a sculptor, at least I could get out and be free again.

The hospital in which I found myself was a small Spanish unit, evidently scraped together from very meagre resources. There was the one Czech doctor, with only four untrained Spanish nurses and two of the walking patients to act as hospital orderlies. There was very little equipment of any sort and the food consisted principally of beans, heavily laced with oil and garlic. My own particular nurse, Sol, worked all day and half the night. On one occasion when she was dressing my hand, she took the sterilized forceps from the jar of alcohol and picked a sterilized dressing out of the drum but unfortunately dropped it on the floor. With her other hand she picked it up, slapped it against her thigh to remove any gross unpleasantness that it had picked up off the floor, blew on it, took it back into the forceps and laid it gently on my wound. She was a dear, sweet girl who was doing her best but I was determined to get myself shifted to the American Hospital as quickly as I could manage it. There was no point in trying to operate through the normal channels of bureaucracy which would take weeks.

After three days I was able to get out of bed and spent all day hanging around the yard looking for an opportunity. Finally it came in the shape of Ray, the American Hospital ambulance driver.

'Ray', I shouted at him.

He came slowly across the yard, peering as if he didn't recognize me. 'Christ what are you doing here?'

'I've been here for three days.'

'But you shouldn't be here. You ought to be over at Villa Paz. Nobody knew what had happened to you.'

'Well, here I am and I want to get out.'

'The hell with that. Jump in,' and he whirled me away before anyone noticed my disappearance.

The American Hospital had moved since I had paid them my overnight visit some months before; they were now at Villa Paz, formerly a summer retreat of the Infanta, only a few miles distant. It was, in essence, a vast farmhouse divided into two huge courtyards, one of which formed the residence while the other dealt with the practicalities of a huge farming area. It was approached by a dirt road winding over the hills of this vast estate of rolling wheatlands, without a building in sight. It was one of the most beautiful areas in the whole of Spain, vast farmlands and wooded country with streams running through it. The billowing fields had no fences or any other division except the road to the two palaces of Villa Paz. It was a large red-brick structure whose only entrance was a huge, arched tunnel driven through the centre of the south wall into a cobbled courtyard about an acre in extent. From here a number of entrances led into the various parts of the building. It was not very palatial, but it did have a most wonderfully calm atmosphere.

I got hold of Freddy Martin and explained that I had no right to be there at all after my illegal escape from the ghastly Spanish hospital at Colmenar. I don't think that Freddy was ever once put off from what she wanted to do, during her whole life. She immediately decided that I should stay, and that I should receive treatment, and that was that.

This new American Hospital at Villa Paz was an entirely different proposition from the make-shift affair that I had visited for a night before I was wounded. The villa had been left untouched since the departure of the Royal Family and American efficiency had turned it into a smoothly operating hospital of about 100 beds with X-ray and pathology labs, operating theatre, modern kitchens and bathrooms. A complete and smooth-working unit of four doctors, twelve nurses and all ancillary services were housed in one building. It also supported a convalescent establishment in another similar minor palace, about a mile away at Saelices. All the medical staff was American, under the leadership of a very large, pompous, and rather aristocratic looking gent. He was reputed to be a senior physician from New England, and the last person one would ever have imagined to have got involved in radical politics. His second in command was a surgeon of about forty-five from Chicago. In addition, there were two young doctors who worked with such tremendous energy and enthusiasm that everybody admired and loved them. They always worked together as a team and seemed to be practically inseparable. The twelve American and two Spanish nurses were headed by Freddy Martin as the indefatigable matron. The ancillary services were all staffed by Americans, with a number of locally recruited Spanish girls engaged in kitchen and general duties. It was a tremendously efficient set up, and although it only had a few patients when I arrived, it later handled thousands of wounded during the Brunete and Belchite campaigns.

I was taken up and put to bed in a large ward on the first floor. I suppose I must have been given a sedative as I went to sleep almost immediately and did not wake up until the middle of the night. I was in a huge hospital ward, but all the beds in my vicinity were empty. Near the foot of the bed sat a nurse reading with a dim light at a small table. She was a fairly tall and very slim girl, sitting in a peculiar position with one upper arm wound around the other supporting her head, and one leg wound around the other to balance herself upon the small chair on which she sat. Her elbows rested on the small table which only had room for the book that she was reading and her lamp. The greater part of the light fell on the book and on her face, and on the two long, entwined hands which supported it. The whole head had a strangely classical and antique quality. A good forehead with strong, black eyebrows and large, dark eyes. A determined nose that could easily have come from a Florentine portrait, high cheek-bones and a firm chin. A largish mouth with a faintly Dionysiac twist at the corners, almost black hair, parted in the centre and drawn back with only the faint sign of a wave, to a small knot low on a long and slender neck. It was a most memorable and striking head, set off by the strangeness of the pose and the character of the light. I realized that I had seen her before on my first crazy visit to the original American hospital, although she had made no particular impression on me at that time. But now I was in a totally different mood. I no longer had to squeeze a lifetime into half-a-dozen hours. I lay cool, clean and relaxed, feeling that time no longer existed.

I must have lain there for some time watching her before she became aware of me. She looked up and unwound herself from the strange position in which she sat and came over to my bed. She was not as tall as I had imagined but very slim and straight, moving with such a loose-limbed walk that it was almost somnambulistic. Her name was Toby, a Hebrew word for a dove. After she had finished the bed straightening, temperature and pulse taking, and the rest of her purely professional duties, I asked if there was any chance of a cup of coffee. She brought two cups, lit a cigarette and put it between the fingers of my left hand, as I could not do it for myself, and sat down on the edge of the bed. We talked for some time: never about the War, but about the way we had lived in peacetime, before the War started. Although she had lived and worked as a nurse in New York city, she was a country girl by origin from a small village way up in the north of Connecticut, where she still kept the original family farmhouse to which she escaped at every possible opportunity. She told me all about this in her strangely deep contralto voice, which contrasted strongly with the delicacy of her appearance. Finally she put me down to sleep, switched off the light, and drifted away to attend to a number of long-term surgical cases who were all at the other end of the ward, and I slept in utter peace and contentment, for the first time in a long while.

After breakfast on the following morning I began to receive the full impact of the hospital organization. First came Freddy and two nurses to clean me up and prepare me for the doctors, who arrived shortly afterwards. They carried out a most exhaustive and exhausting scrutiny of my entire physical condition. This was followed by a long session in the X-ray room where various photos of my head, left arm and right hand were taken. After this I was put back to bed and left to rest. During the evening, various of my friends came to visit me and it was quite a festive occasion. Later, when everybody had left, Toby and I had another coffee and cigarette session. We were now much more self-conscious with one another than on the previous night. We talked for a long time as if there was some urgent necessity to establish links with one another as quickly as possible. Finally she gave me a very chaste kiss and I went to sleep.

I was not allowed breakfast on the following morning and this ominous sign was followed by a visit from the two young doctors and the surgeon from Chicago. They had the X-ray plates with them and, with that infuriating detachment of surgeons, they proceeded to examine and discuss my situation in the most purely academic manner as if I, as a person, did not exist. They quickly decided that the damage to my left thumb was a nerve injury which could be depended on to correct itself in the course of time. The plate of my right hand showed a fracture of the fourth metacarpal bone and an extensive shattering of the fifth. In addition, the whole plate was covered with small black specks of different shapes and sizes, which indicated pieces of the bullet. Everybody seemed to agree that they were so numerous that any attempt to remove them would do more harm than good, and that they would eventually become encapsulated and cause no real trouble. Most of the pieces in my head did not appear to be a cause of worry, but some of those in and around my eyes would have to be removed and this was a rather terrifying prospect.

They shaved and scrubbed me, dressed me in peculiar garments, placed me on what looked suspiciously like a funeral bier, and wheeled me away to the operating theatre. I was filled with horror by the whole affair but there didn't seem to be anything to do about it. Then followed the anaesthetic and the nightmare dreams, until I woke up, for the second time with my head all tied up in bandages, unable to see or to use either hand. Locked up in darkness I went through another period of shock and trauma until one of the nurses came along and settled me down so that I was able to sleep again. When I awoke for the second time I felt perfectly calm and knew that Toby was somewhere close at hand. She must have seen me move and put her hand on my shoulder. 'Don't worry. They've done a swell job on you and everything's going to be just fine.'

'How can they know that?'

'It seems that there was no damage to the optic nerve and none of the small pieces of metal did any real harm. They've taken some of them out and the rest are harmless.'

'You mean my eyesight's going to be all right?'

'Sure it is.'

'How long do I have to wear these God-damned bandages all over my face?'

'Only two or three days. Then you'll be fine.'

'Toby, my love, I'm sorry to be such a mess.'

'Don't worry. It won't be long. But now go back to sleep and I'll bring you a cup of coffee before I go off in the morning.'

A few days later the bandages were removed and sure enough I could see perfectly. The only moment of horror came when I happened to see my face in the mirror. I had been given a prison hair-cut, eye-brows and lashes had disappeared, my skin was distorted by reason of the stitches, and the whole mess was made more horrible by peeling areas of red and yellow medications. My face looked positively obscene and the thought of going through life with that awful distorted and blotched appearance was a thing of horror. There was no need for this ridiculous trauma: if someone had warned me that I looked a mess at the moment, but that the whole thing would return to normality in a few days, I would not have been so upset. I had seen rather too much of the mutilation of the human form during the last few months, and I was over-sensitive on the subject.

The damage to my left thumb was caused by a superficial wound in the bicep which had affected the nerve controlling my thumb. It was not painful but the thumb was completely numb and I could not use it. I was told that the nerve would gradually reconstitute itself. This proved to be true, but even now my left thumb is still slightly numb although its use had not been seriously impaired for many years. The problem of my right hand was more complicated. The two outer bones in the palm of my hand were completely smashed. I would have to reconcile myself to the fact that for practical purposes, I would only be able to use two fingers and the thumb of my right hand. It might have all been a good deal worse. The one serious aspect of the thing was that I clearly would not be able to continue to work as a sculptor, and I did not know what the hell else I wanted, or would be able, to do.

I was now convinced that the War could not possibly be won and that its continuation would only result in useless slaughter. The trouble was that we were riding the back of a tiger and there was no way to get off. The Republican Government had been perfectly correct in trying to

defend itself against the military uprising which had sought to destroy
it, but it now became increasingly plain that the War was lost. It was all
very fine for the 'left' of Europe and America to beat their breasts and
demand that the common people of Spain should fight to the last man,
but this was as brutal and irresponsible as the mob shouting for blood at
the Roman circus. Once it had become apparent that the War could not
be won it should have been terminated.

From a purely military standpoint we were out-gunned and out-
thought. Franco had the trained professional soldiers and the overwhelming superiority of technical equipment. Moorish infantry
supported by German artillery, Italian tanks and aircraft in bewildering
quantities, might be held down by the fanatical heroism of the workers'
battalions in street fighting, as they had been at Madrid, but when it
came to set-piece battles we were no match for them. Madrid still held,
but the northern sectors – Basque, Galicia and Asturias – had been
over-run, with the result that Franco could now concentrate his entire
force on the Central Fronts.

Politically speaking the situation had become desperate. Azana as
President had proved as indecisive as he had been when Prime Minister.
The Government in Valencia no longer had any pretence to being the
representative of the will of the people. Largo Caballero, whose
premiership had more or less been accepted by all the factions of the
Left, had been forced to resign as he would not agree to the destruction
of the POUM. The Government was totally dependent on Russia for
its supply of arms with the result that the Communist Party had total
control of the political structure within the Republic. Negrin, whose
very name was totally unknown to the mass of the people, was appointed
Prime Minister on the instructions of the Party. He was an intellectual
and a man of extreme arrogance. Nominally a member of the Socialist
Party, and a deputy for several years, he played no active role in politics
until Largo Caballero had called him in as Minister of Finance in
September 1936. He was a man of the *grande bourgeoisie* and certainly no
Communist, but he admired the ruthlessness of the Communist Party
policies and thought that he could use them as a tool to centralize the
diverse elements in the Republic and bring them into a single planned
and efficient unit. It was typical of his arrogance that he believed that
he was making use of the Communist Party when, in fact, they were

using him. It was agreed between them that the Trades Union movement – both CNT and UGT – were to be united, whether they liked
it or not. There was to be no further talk of the Revolution. All political
parties were to be strictly subservient to the central Government. We
were now fighting solely for the Republic and there must not be any
kind of action or propaganda that would upset bourgeois sensibilities.
The process of land reforms was to be halted and assistance denied to
the co-operatives. Everything that the mass of the Republicans thought
that they were fighting for was cancelled out.

Personally, there was nothing more that I could do about it. I was
tolerably sure that the medical board in Albacete would order my
repatriation as being unfit for further military service and I should be
pleased to go. The whole show had gone sour and there was no longer
any hope of sweetening it again. I was desperately sorry for the Spanish
people and the shameful way in which they had been misused. It was a
ghastly situation, meeting and talking to all the sweet and friendly
Spanish people working around the hospital, while knowing the fate
which would be their lot at Franco's hands, in payment for all the kind-
ness and generosity which they were showing to us. Even after thirty
years the horror of that situation hangs around me like the odour of
sour and decomposing milk. I hadn't achieved very much on their
behalf and if I could achieve nothing more, it was time to leave.

I stayed in Villa Paz for about six weeks and inevitably I fell in love.
It was glorious weather and the setting of the building was one of the
prettiest that I have seen in the whole of Spain. Open, rolling country
with plenty of large trees, a small river burbling its way through large
round boulders. There were very few patients at the time since the
Lincoln Battalion had been largely inactive for so long and most of those
who were there were the very seriously wounded from the original
battles at Jarama in February – men with their arms in huge 'aeroplane'
splints which stuck out like the arms of a semaphore apparatus, poor
devils lying in bed with a mass of pulleys and weights to hold their
broken bones into position. Others who had suffered wounds which had
mangled their flesh around broken bones were totally sealed into plaster
cases which stank like the wrath of hell when they were opened. One
unfortunate, Robert Raven, became a sort of propaganda show-piece.
His face was completely smashed. His eyes and lips were gone, but he

still managed to talk reasonably well, and it was truly frightening to hear a more or less normal voice coming out of the small hole in the scaly, pink mass of what had been a face. His hands and legs were almost entirely useless and yet, despite it all, he always seemed bright and cheerful, which only added to the horror of it. He was a 'must' on the itinerary of all the tourists. He was brave and stupid and said all the right things that the propaganda machine wanted him to say. It was really disgusting to see this poor benighted piece of human wreckage being made use of as a propaganda mouthpiece. It was not even as if the poor bastard had done anything heroic: he had simply blown himself up with a hand-grenade out of pure stupidity. But this piece of information was strictly concealed. The Party needed a hero and poor, unfortunate Raven happened to be the only piece of available human material for the job.

Toby and I became deeply involved with one another as the days passed and, logically and inevitably, we became lovers. But I was up against something that had never happened to me before or since. I became obsessed with the idea of producing a child. Sex developed an entirely new dimension and we were untiring in our pursuit of it. Something had to be done about the situation and one afternoon when Stephanovitch, the Brigade Intelligence Officer, came over on a visit, we co-opted him and his car, Freddy Martin, and a few others, to go and find some official who would legally marry us. But the whole thing seemed to be quite hopeless. There had been no law of civil marriage before the War, and now there were no priests, and neither of us would have wanted them if they had existed. The prospect of two atheists going through the pretence of a religious marriage in front of a fat and corrupt priest appealed to nobody. It is perfectly true that there were honest and decent priests in Spain but they were few and far between, so that one's vision of priests in general had become corrupted by the general pattern. The civil bureaucracy was in such chaos that no mayor or other official seemed to know what his powers were or what the procedure was and finally we gave up.

But if we could not have an official marriage I decided to invent one that would satisfy me, if nobody else. The farm had a wonderful two-wheeled cart and a pair of most beautiful, creamy, long-horned oxen. The whole affair looked as if it had survived intact from ancient Athens,

specially devised for some Dionysiac celebration. We garlanded the
oxen with wreaths of flowers, loaded the cart with a barrel of wine and
an assortment of food stuffs and set off to hold a feast. Nearby there was
a stream with a small cascade, set in a copse of trees. Everybody off
duty joined us: we ate, drank, splashed around in the water and caressed
the sweet, docile oxen, all in the dappled shade of the surrounding
trees. Finally we wandered home singing and leading the oxen. Toby
and I retired to bed amid the plaudits of our friends. All of which was
probably as good a method of getting married as any other.

At this stage we started to hear a lot about the 'New Army'. The
slogan under which it was to be constituted was that everyone should
forget their regional or political differences and concentrate on winning
the War; after which the various political parties would hammer out
a new constitution which would satisfy everybody. Superficially this
sounded like common sense – in reality it was the most palpable nonsense. Galicia, Basque and Catalonia each had a large and determined
organization pledged to independence of a unified Spanish State. The
Anarchist Confederation, which was one of the largest political groups
in Spain, utterly refused to participate in any elections to a central
Government. The Republican and Liberal Parties were pledged to a
reformed capitalist state with a constitution similar to that of Great
Britain or the United States of America. The vast majority were in
favour of social justice and education without any very clear notions of
a political method of achieving this purpose. Above all, the destruction
of the POUM and the execution of its leaders by the Communist Party
had created an atmosphere of mutual suspicion between political factions which was incurable under the existing circumstances. Too many
people were seeing any tendency to disagree with the official line as
wilful treason and an attempt to create divisions for the benefit of the
enemy. Spy-fever became rife, a great number of secret trials and executions were taking place, and every man was becoming suspicious of
his neighbour.

In the early days the workers' militia units had been organized on the
basis of political groupings which resulted in each unit having a common
cause. There must have been endless and acrimonious disputes at
Brigade and Divisional levels between representatives of the various
political factions. But, at last, there was a sound and enthusiastic morale

amongst the rank and file. The New Army concept eliminated all the volunteer units, based on political and local allegiances. All were to be merged into a general conscript army which – theoretically – had no particular political basis other than the defence of the Republic against the Fascist revolt. This attempted rationalization might have made sense in some countries, but to deprive Spaniards of partisanship was totally destructive of their morale.

On the face of it, nobody could reasonably quarrel with the concept of the New Army as an attempt to shelve all internal divisions with the single aim of uniting to fight the common enemy, In practice it was not so innocent. The units which accepted the principle were heavily reinforced with men and equipment. It was obvious that those which were most ready to accept the principle were those in which the Communist Party and their allies were in the majority, since the concept derived from the Party, with the result that the Communists controlled the largest and most heavily armed units. The POUM militia had already been disarmed after the uproar in Barcelona in May; their leaders had been arrested and many of them executed. A number of other militia units belonging to the Anarchist and other parties began to suspect that they were due for the same treatment. The New Army Political Commissars were all Communist-trained, and this new dispensation virtually meant that there would be a conscript army under Communist control, from platoon level upwards. All the fine old slogans about the masses taking up arms and leaping to the defence of the Republic were going to become so much nonsense and the War was going to boil down to a straight-out fight between Franco and the Communists, who had never been able to muster more than a few thousand supporters in the whole of Spain. But they always held the whip hand over any Government in power in the Republic, because the USSR was the only source of arms and ammunition available to it and Russia was not going to support any government which it did not control.

Shortly after I was wounded our whole Brigade had been withdrawn from Jarama and reconstructed. It now consisted of six reconstituted battalions, divided into two sections, all under the command of Copic. The British and the Lincolns had been brought up to full strength and an entirely new American Battalion, the George Washington, had been formed to complete the first section. This was under the command of George Nathan. The second section consisted of the reconstructed Dimitrov and Franco-Belge Battalions, together with a Spanish Battalion. These formed part of the army of 50,000 which included many of the best Brigades in the Republican Army, supported by 150 aircraft, 125 tanks and 136 pieces of artillery, which was to take part in the first Government offensive to be launched at Brunete on 6th July. The purpose of the attack was to drive back or cut off Franco's position in the Western suburbs of Madrid, from whence his artillery was able to disrupt industry and to terrorize the population. The whole affair was hopelessly mismanaged from the start and the battle continued until 26th July by which time the Republican troops were driven back, almost to their original lines. Half of the original number of troops were dead, and half of the equipment lost. The British Battalion was reduced to platoon strength. The Lincoln and Washington Battalions were amalgamated, but still formed less than one Battalion in numerical strength. Nathan and Oliver Law, the negro in command of the Washingtons were killed, and Martin Hourihan was so badly wounded that he was invalided out. For the moment, at least, the Republic was rendered incapable of making a further offensive.

There were a tremendous number of casualties as a result of this battle and orders were received at Villa Paz to evacuate any wounded man who was capable of walking to make room for the men from Brunete. The ambulances started to arrive that evening, and a ghastly sight it was. They were all loaded up with six to eight men in various states of injury. They had travelled over bad roads for about seventy miles and a number of them were already dead. They were lifted out of the ambulances on the stretchers in which they lay, and were set out in rows on the cobblestones of the courtyard. The ambulances themselves were quickly washed out and immediately set off for the battle-front again to collect another consignment. I now heard that Marty was amongst those who had been wounded and would probably be brought down with the next load. But it was no use me hanging around any longer – I could be of no service and should only be in the way.

Villa Paz had become the centre of my life. Apart from the fact that it contained a number of dear and intimate friends, together with my newly acquired wife, it represented a haven of peace and safety in an exceedingly unsafe world. However, the moment had finally arrived when I should have to leave. The only uniform that I could find was one of the wretched-looking cotton corduroy battle-dresses, a pair of rope-soled *alpagata* shoes, and a shirt, as well as a razor and toothbrush. This wasn't very much of an outfit, but the weather was now warm and dry so that it would serve well enough. By a series of miracles I had still been able to hang on to my passport; I carried a letter from the Hospital to the Medical Board in Albacete, recommending my discharge and repatriation; I had a fair stock of pesetas for immediate expenses, and I borrowed $100 to cover my situation if I got out of Spain. My friends all joined me for a farewell drink at the little bar under the gateway and I felt very blue indeed as Ray took me down to Tarancón, where I picked up a lift to Albacete.

13

The Last Lap

In Albacete I signed in to the Guardia Civil Barracks which I had left the previous January as a very raw recruit. Even at that time the barracks had been pretty dreary and unclean but now they were truly dreadful. The blankets and bedding were dirty and infested with lice, the lavatories a welter of filth, and the food abominable. There was no mail and no cigarettes. A few of the residents were newly arrived recruits waiting to be posted to their units, but the majority were old friends who had been wounded at Jarama and discharged from hospital, some for the second time, many of them with their wounds only partially healed, on crutches, strung up on aeroplane splints, or blind. All the hospitals had been hurriedly emptied of the mobile wounded to make room for the flood of casualties from the battle of Brunete.

Theoretically, every man had to attend a Medical Board after his discharge from hospital. The Board would then classify him as fit to return to service, fit for non-combatant service, or unfit for any form of military service with an order for their repatriation. Waiting for examination by the board, and for its subsequent findings, developed in us all a nerve-racking sense of insecurity about our future. In addition, there was always the danger that some bureaucrat would descend on the barracks and arbitrarily decide that some of us were fit enough for service and order us back to our Battalion. All this uncertainty, together with the squalid condition of life, had reduced morale to a pretty low ebb. Nobody was concerned about our well-being, while Vidal and his clique, who were supposed to be in charge of the place, still lounged idly around the guard-room, as impudent as ever. Nothing had changed since I had passed through the place in January. There was no officer or Political Commissar among us, and because I had been on the Brigade staff, the others looked to me to try and do something to alleviate the situation. I wanted no part in it whatsoever.

Albacete, at this time, was full of Party bureaucrats of all shapes and sizes. They were immediately recognizable by their black leather jackets, Sam Browne belts with large automatic pistols, and huge black berets, in emulation of their master, André Marty. They were all infected with spy-fever and everyone knew that there was a Russian KGB prison and interrogation centre somewhere in the neighbourhood. On the slightest hint of subversion or 'Trotskyism' – which might include almost anything – a man was likely to disappear and never be seen again. Vidal was generally supposed to be a senior Communist functionary, and so he must have been to have been able to get away with so much for so long. In these circumstances, any complaint against him was liable to be construed as an attack on the Communist Party itself, something which immediately came under the heading of Trotskyism.

The only constructive action I could suggest taking for the moment was that we should parade ourselves in the yard as cleanly and neatly turned out as possible, and so draw attention to ourselves as an orderly, disciplined body in marked contrast to the rest of the men in the barracks. We asked for soap, buckets, scrubbing-brushes and so forth to try and clean up our own section of the barracks, and discovered a privately-owned wash-house in the town where, for a few pesetas, it was possible to get a bath and wash our clothing. We paraded ourselves twice a day and prepared a nominal rota, with dates of attendance at the Medical Board and other particulars. All this activity was rather heavily frowned on, but we had done nothing against which official action could be taken. However, suspicion began to grow that we were a subversive influence and that it would be a good thing if we were dispersed. Draft chits started to appear with increasing frequency as the bureaucracy of the Medical Board ground into action under the stimulus of a higher authority, and our numbers had been reduced to about fifty when we received a visit from Harry Pollitt, the head man of the British Communist Party.

I had never seen Pollitt at close quarters before. He was a smallish, balding individual, with small dark eyes that looked as though he had never smiled in his life. He was neatly dressed in a city suit with collar and tie. We had been warned that he was coming to see us and everybody was full of the expectation that he would bring a message of encouragement and joy. On the contrary. He had evidently come down with the express purpose of bawling us out. The general line of his argument was that we needn't think that, because we had served in the Battalion and had been wounded, anybody owed us anything. Quite the reverse, we had been given the opportunity to serve in this glorious cause and that should be enough for anyone. How dare we complain that we were not getting mail and cigarettes? – we were lucky enough to have been in the Battalion at all. Let us not think that we were in the vanguard of the revolutionary struggle. Far from it, we were merely the raw material, while the real revolutionary workers slaved night and day in the Party offices to bring about the millennium. He followed this up with a number of vague threats against shirkers and malingerers; and then left. It had been quite a performance.

Fear and suspicion tempered the whole of life in Albacete. The Party bureaucrats were under the continual dread of being sent to the Front, although this was presumably what they had come to Spain for in the first place. The demented figure of André Marty hung over us all. Nobody knew where or when he was liable to put in an appearance, and all sorts of rumours circulated of the executions he had ordered for little or no reason at all. I don't suppose anyone will ever know the truth of the whole matter, but it was an extremely unpleasant atmosphere to live in. Throughout my time in the International Brigades morale was always in a perilous condition and yet, amazingly enough, nobody in authority ever seemed to realize that pep talks and threats were no substitute for cleanliness, reasonable food, and football or some other form of light, active entertainment. As it was, the men just sat around grumbling in dirt and idleness.

For myself, I decided to keep my own company and stayed away from the barracks as much as possible. I walked for miles all around the town, and during my wanderings I discovered various small bars where I could get odd snacks of food with a glass of wine, so that I was not dependent on the vile swill offered by the barracks. The roast potato seller was a favourite stopping place – a large potato split up the middle, with a dollop of olive oil and a little salt, washed down with half a litre of rough wine, served me very well for a complete meal. There was only one restaurant in town that was still operating and this was strictly the preserve of the Party elite, but on the whole I managed quite comfortably.

Finally I received an order to report at the Medical Tribunal, which turned out to be one elderly, French doctor. He looked at my papers from Villa Paz, gave me a superficial examination and marked my red card as unfit for further military service. This was the first and most decisive step. I then was directed to another office where, after an extensive cross-examination, I was given a paper which stated that I should be repatriated. One of the major problems all along the line was that we had never been issued with identity cards, so that one had to prove one's identity under interrogation at each stage of the game. Finally I received a military pass to proceed by rail to Valencia, Barcelona and the border at Port Bou. One of the periodical clean-outs was going on at the barracks so, taking no chances, I headed straight for the station and found a place on the overnight train. We rattled through the valley and into Valencia in the early hours of the morning. Practically all trains were routed during the hours of darkness, owing to the danger of air raids and coastal bombardment; consequently I had a whole day to pass in the city until the next stage of my journey. I had a bad moment when I was arrested by a patrol at the station, but the sergeant in the station police office stamped my papers and let me go in peace.

The town looked very neglected and depressing in this, the second year of the Civil War. However, I found my way out to a little booth-restaurant on a beach outside the town. The family who ran it were very kind to me. I ate great quantities of fish – a food I had not seen in a long time – drank good wine, slept on the beach, and idled the day away until it was time to go and catch my train. Another miserable night on the unrelenting wooden benches of a third-class carriage of a blacked-out train: and so to Barcelona.

Barcelona in August was vastly different to what it had been in December. There were far fewer people in the street. The parades with bands and banners had all gone. The euphoric revolutionary enthusiasm had disappeared and everybody seemed to be minding their own business. Most of the shops and restaurants were closed and even the nightlife had become subdued. I was obliged to go up to the old Artillery Barracks – now the Karl Marx Barracks – in order to get my *salvo conducto* to cross the border at Port Bou. It was no secret that there were a number of deserters and others trying to get out of the country and the security check would become increasingly fierce as I got nearer to the border. I hung around the barracks for three days getting shuffled around from one office to another, constantly afraid that when I handed over my papers for examination, I would not get them back. The reason for all this pointless apprehension was the attitude of the various interrogating officers who treated me with such a degree of suspicion that I began to feel like a fugitive. In fact, my papers were in perfectly good order; I had a clear discharge as a soldier who had served the Republic and was now too badly wounded to be of further value. I did not expect to be made much of, but I was getting sick of being treated like a criminal. Finally I received a document which entitled me to cross the border at Port Bou and a third-class ticket to Paris. There was no train until late that night but eventually we were on our way. The train stopped at every station and was constantly invaded by armed police, checking everybody's papers. I had to stand in line for hours at Port Bou but in the end I got back aboard the train and we rumbled through the tunnel to Cerbère and into France.

I was now able to produce my passport from its place of concealment inside my shirt and to recover my identity without having to prove who I was by a process of interrogation. Only a handful of people were crossing the border and the French immigration officials passed me through without comment. I got off the train at Cerbère. I was now safely out of Spain, and free of the possibility that some villainous-looking member of the secret police might tap me on the shoulder and start the whole nightmare over again. I was out of trouble and I wanted to savour the feel of it.

I was still dressed in the thin, khaki cotton corduroy jacket and trousers and the *alpagata* shoes of the International Brigades and carried no possessions of any kind except my passport, a third-class ticket to Paris, my Spanish papers and some money. I had worn these clothes for so long that it did not occur to me that I must have looked rather peculiar in a French village during the holiday season. Usually the men from Spain stayed on the train until it got to Paris, so I would have been completely unidentifiable to the locals – or so, at least, I imagined. The town was full of French petit bourgeois holiday makers, who were methodically enjoying their annual break as economically as possible, without worrying much about anyone else.

The whole tempo of life in France, even the smell of French cafés, was utterly different from anything in Spain, and for the time being I enjoyed every moment of it. Even the impossible egocentricity of the French appeared to be totally charming. I bought the first decent packet of cigarettes I had had in a long time and strolled slowly through the town, savouring the sight of a great variety of shops which actually had something to sell. The plethora of every possible kind of merchandise was intoxicating after life in Spain where the shops kept open – more from habit, than for any other reason – with little or nothing on sale. Here there were cheerful groups of animated men and women filling the streets instead of the crowds of dirty, bored men in uniform. It was going to take a lot of effort to fit myself back into normal life again.

Finally I came to a café with a terrace overlooking the harbour. It looked very gay with its little tables and bright-coloured umbrellas, and a wonderful view extending for miles across the country beyond the bay. It was still too early for the café to have many customers and I had the place almost entirely to myself. I ordered *café crème*, croissants, butter and jam: it seemed to be the most delicious meal I have ever eaten. I ate the lot, lay back in my chair and smoked a cigarette, ordered a second consignment, and finished that. My mind had hardly been functioning at all until now. But the food, the quietness of the place and the tranquillity of the view calmed down my nerves so that I was at last able to take stock of the last nine months and everything that had happened to me.

It didn't feel like nine months since I had walked into Robson's office in King Street, it felt like as many years. I had hated the whole business but I did not regret it. There had been a certain inevitability about it from start to finish. Given the sort of person that I was, it was inevitable that I should have joined the International Brigades in the first place: it was all part of the rather naive, romantic idealism that had made me a radical. Looking back over the thing, I now began to realize how incredibly lucky I had been. I had survived the initial shambles at Jarama. George Nathan had roped me in to the Brigade staff, and the polyglots had looked after me when I was in no position to look after myself. I had received a wound severe enough to be invalided out of Spain only a few weeks before the massacre of the Lincoln Battalion at Brunete. Through my friends at the American Hospital, and the care that they had lavished on me, I was not going to suffer any irretrievable injury. Finally I had found myself a beautiful wife that I adored. It might have been a hell of a lot worse.

Later on, when I arrived back in London, I found that my mother and all my friends had heard that I had been killed. There had been no official confirmation, which was not surprising as there was not even a system of registering next of kin. Relatives and friends of the men in Spain were entirely dependent for news on gossip or reports from those who had been invalided out and returned home. This peculiarly heartless attitude was typical of the lack of concern exercised by the bureaucrats of King Street – they could not see the necessity for even the most elementary welfare service. It was the Party's business to send men out to fight in the International Brigades but it did not bother itself with what happened to them subsequently. My future prospects were – to say the least of it – unpromising. There was clearly no possibility of continuing my career as a sculptor or in any other manual trade, and I had no idea in the world what I wanted, or was able, to do in its place.

However, the whole thing was behind me now and the nightmare was over. All the friends that I had made were dead or, for one reason or another, I was never to see again. There is no longer any point in trying to untangle the web of lies and confusions which lay behind that ghastly Civil War. It arose out of total confusion and chaos. There were individuals on both sides who committed every possible form of cruelty and beastliness. And nobody, from either side, came out of it with clean hands. We, of the International Brigades, had wilfully deluded ourselves into the belief that we were fighting a noble Crusade because we needed a crusade – the opportunity to fight against the manifest evils of Fascism, in one form or another, which seemed then as if it would overwhelm every value of Western civilization. We were wrong, we deceived ourselves and were deceived by others: but even then, the whole thing was not in vain. Even at the moments of the greatest gloom and depression, I have never regretted that I took part in it. The situation is not to be judged by what we now know of it, but only as it appeared in the context of the period. And in that context there was a clear choice for anyone who professed to be opposed to Fascism. The fact that others took advantage of our idealism in order to destroy it does not in any way invalidate the decision which we made.

The last word lies with the speech of Dolores Ibarruri – *La Pasionaria* – fish peddler, miner's widow and Member of Parliament, made at the final stand-down parade of the International Brigades at Barcelona on 15th November, 1938.

'Mothers! Women! When the years pass by and the wounds of war are staunched: when the cloudy memory of the sorrowful, bloody days returns in a present of freedom, love, and well-being: when the feelings of rancour are dying away and when pride in a free country is felt equally by all Spaniards – then speak to your children. Tell them of the International Brigades. Tell them how, coming over seas and mountains, crossing frontiers bristling with bayonets, and watched for by ravening dogs thirsty to tear at their flesh, these men reached our country as Crusaders for freedom. They gave up everything, their loves, their country, home and fortune – fathers, mothers, wives, brothers, sisters and children and they came and told us: "We are here, your cause, Spain's cause, is ours. It is the cause of all advanced and progressive mankind." Today they are going away. Many of them, thousands of them, are staying here with the Spanish earth for their shroud, and all Spaniards remember them with the deepest feeling.'

Then she addressed the assembled members of the Brigades.

'Comrades of the International Brigades! Political reasons, reasons of State, the welfare of that same cause for which you offered your blood with boundless generosity, are sending you back, some of you to your own countries and others to forced exile. You can go proudly. You are history. You are legend. You are the heroic example of democracy's solidarity and universality. We shall not forget you, and when the olive tree of peace puts forth its leaves again, mingled with the laurels of the Spanish Republic's victory – come back!'